# THAT
# ROOT
## YOU LEFT BEHIND

**SAMUEL A. BENTUM (Ph.D)**

Order this book online at www.trafford.com
or email orders@trafford.com

Most Trafford titles are also available at major online book retailers.

Print information available on the last page.

ISBN: 978-1-4907-8685-8 (sc)
ISBN: 978-1-4907-8687-2 (hc)
ISBN: 978-1-4907-8686-5 (e)

Library of Congress Control Number: 2018900080

**Manuscript Editor:** Eric Kwadwo Amissah
**Illustrator/Sculptor/Collector:** Samuel Adentwi Bentum
**Graphic Designer/Photographer:** Ernest Doe Kudjorjie
**Cover Page Design:** Ernest Doe Kudjorjie

*Trafford rev. 01/28/2020*

Trafford
PUBLISHING®  www.trafford.com
**North America & international**
toll-free: 1 888 232 4444 (USA & Canada)
fax: 812 355 4082

# ACKNOWLEDGEMENTS

Greater thanks go to my sisters Phillipa and Beryl with whom I owe much of my sustenance of good health and to Auntie Essiah of Ngyeresia Payin, Sekondi, who helped in the location and transporting of some of these wonderful discarded tree roots.

My sincere thanks go to Eric Kwadwo Amissah who tactfully edited and co-ordinated the writing activity and Frederick N. Anderson for his financial interventions.

Ernest Doe Kudjordjie who took photographs of the found and fixed pieces, designed and finally, turned the manuscripts and photographs into a book.

To all those who criticized, encouraged and moved the thoughts into another level culminating to this book, I am grateful and appreciate all their efforts.

# DEDICATION

I totally and wholly dedicate this book to the farmers and people of Ngeresia Payin, Sekondi, from whom these collections of discarded tree roots were obtained.

# TABLE OF CONTENTS

# LIST OF PLATES

# LIST OF FIGURES

# FOREWORD

Many Africans have a sober observation of environmental art and as a result have ignored the rewards and ideals thereof. However, there is adequate evidence to show that the environment that the artist lives in and the socio-cultural and political lives of the artist shape the quality, purity and standard of his rendition.

Bentum's book, That Root You Left Behind expresses his creative energy in contemporary African sculpture dimensions. His found and fixed root-works explain some concepts that support the African social, secular, political and economic influences – a relation of a real life situation and obscurity.

Although, these sculptured pieces are but simple, they depict the African background stuffed with respect for divine interventions and favour from the benevolent and the unseen. Bentum's collection of his sketches and sculptures shows a sense of adoption, steadiness and excellent treatment of discarded pieces.

That Root You Left Behind is the kind of book most people in Africa and elsewhere should read in order to be conversant with African art in the context of the ideals of tenacity, passion, support and mystery.

**SAM–ACKAH ODEYEMI**
(Art Critic, Former Dean of Students Affairs,
Former Head, Department of Liberal Studies,
Takoradi Technical University,
Takoradi, Ghana.)

## PREFACE

That Root You Left Behind—Champions of Hope Series—touches on the Aesthetics and Appreciation of discarded Tree Roots into inspirational art forms. That Root You Left Behind also brings into perspective an aspect which allows appreciation and understanding of art in relation to real-life situations. In the distant past, and even till now, artists' inspirational and motivational exponents have relied on nature and the environment as the prime mode of motivation, expression and artistry. Discarded tree roots are comparable sculptural medium that can be identified and fixed for visual appreciation and acceptance. Nature, in this sense, expresses the aesthetics of the forms that hitherto exists within these discarded tree roots that litter the communities and our environment

That Root You Left Behind is a compilation of real-life visual illustrations that projects the sequence of lifetime stories of persons who have achieved prominence from a poor or bad start to the lime light. These illustrations are without a single stroke of line or a movement of dot. They are mental projections and illustrations about people who were affluent from the beginning of their lives, but became lost in their comfort zones. Hence, the dignity of the human culture is clearly and sturdily time-honoured through the form and imagery naturally created from these tree roots. Titles of these root sculptures were derived from the Champion Series collections.

The surfaces of these roots scheme some root bark textures, surface defects and marks from chain saw, machete and blade of earth moving machines The stories behind these collections are centred on real-life experiences of being rejected today and being honoured tomorrow. This gives hope to the hopeless— a situation which establishes that favour is able to turn round the destiny of mankind. Like the Bible story – *The Stone the Builders Rejected has become the Head Corner Stone of the Building.*

**SAMUEL ADENTWI BENTUM** (Ph.D)

# INTRODUCTION

A re-broadcast of his message on a popular radio station in Takoradi, inspired his listeners by stating; Take God First and He Will Take You To Places You Never Dreamt Of – JOEL OSTEN. I posted this statement on my Facebook_wall and it attracted thousands of my followers who were equally astonished and inspired by this great and wise saying.

In our everyday's dealings, whether with mankind or cosmic, we encounter some degrees of non-expectance and non-acceptance due to the necessary defects and dictates that leads or follows us as we journey through life. The principles' of rejection, dejection and ejection which manifests in reject—refuse, rebuff, decline, snub, betray, throw out, discard, disallow, eliminate or deject—discourage, dishearten, depress, demoralize, disparage, make unhappy and eject— throw out, cast out, expel, get rid of, emit, drive out, show somebody the door and banish are some negatives sure to confront us in all our lives facades.

In the natural sense, all humans do presume and anticipate good wishes, good omen and better path to life's journey. On the contrary, the principle of Injection—inject, insert, bring in, add, introduce, instil and infuse, bounces our destiny to bond with that of the Creator.

Tree roots are the foundations upon which the tree trunks, tree branches and leaves and fruits take their physical strength and nourishment. Tree roots anchor trees into the soil and as well assist in the mineral transfer from the soil to the tree leaves and convey photosynthesis (sun energy) from the leaves to the roots heads. Some tree roots serves as food source to both human and animal. Tree roots provide the needed essential minerals and nutrients required for both human and animal sustainability.

In a larger extent, tree roots are known to provide the necessary medicinal components needed for human and animal wellbeing. In recent times, tree roots have become a major component for alcoholic and non-alcoholic beverages in Ghana and other West African countries.

A typical example is the Ruut Special— a cassava root beverage brewed in Ghana by Guinness Ghana Limited and also the Orijin, herbal beverage also brewed in Ghana by Guinness Ghana Limited. There are several breweries today in Ghana that rely on tree roots. These breweries provide numerous employments both in the manufacturing and the supply chain value to the teeming youth of Ghana. Tree roots have also become a major source of medication for the traditional African Medical Practitioners. There is no single private commercial passenger coach where one will not witness the advertisement and sales of one type or another herbal medicine from tree parts. Additionally, it is eluded that, some greater spiritual potency displaced by some traditional priests, priestesses and medicine men are derived from the spiritual efficacy that inhibits these tree parts—tree roots.

## Sources of Tree Roots

Tree roots are usually that part of the tree that has minimal commercial and economic value as compare to tree trunks, branches, leaves and fruits. Tree roots are usually hidden in their surrounding soil, except some species that have their parts exposed above the soil. Such trees roots include that of mangrove, Cotton tree and other buttress tree roots. Tree roots are usually obtained through several sources. Tree roots may be identified and collected from the soil, the surface of earth–streets and road sides and sites, domestic compounds, industrial and commercial environments, constructional sites, tree plantation and forest. These sources include farm lands and farming activity sites, building sites and building construction sites, road sides and road construction sites, river beds and river banks, lagoons and sea shores.

Attempts at clearing farm lands for farming, clearing building sites for domestic and residential facilities, clearing lands for road construction and road expansion expose several tree roots and stumps. Dredging of river beds and streams, channelling of streams and rivers ways also provide additional source for the acquisition of tree roots. In some situations, tree roots are exposed to the environment through the activities of nature and man. In certain communities and neighbourhood where the soil is not protected, excessive soil erosion overly exposed the tree roots. These may weaken the foundation of the tree therefore falling them at the least provocation of the wind or storm. This book focuses on discarded tree parts—tree roots taken from farmlands, constructional sites, industrial premises and residential compounds within the Sekondi- Takoradi Metropolis.

## Formation of Tree Roots Shapes and Forms

The shape and form of a tree's roots are dependent upon the ecology of its existence. Tree roots from temperate regions are noted to have a divergent representation from that of the tropical regions. Likewise, tree roots from forest zones have variance representation in shape and form as compared to that of savannah and coastal belts. It is imperative that the soil composition and formation has greater influence on the root formation. Stony soil reacts differently to that of the clayey type. Equally, soggy soil has different response to that of a dry-hard soil. It is true that soils may determine the formation of tree roots; it is worth noting that particular species of tree lend themselves to particular root formation. Examples are the mangrove and silk cotton trees.

## Tree Roots – Science and Environment

As a contribution to the world of art, this book seeks to add knowledge to the approaches of addressing the menace of the environment through environmental cleaning which is in line with the production of these environmental sculptures. This is done through the careful selection and fixing of these natural objects and forms–discarded tree roots as raw materials for the production of artworks. Sculpture in wood that engages tree parts constitute a greater percentage of wood sculpture in Ghana and West Africa.

Nature in her cyclical sequence naturally has a way of scientifically dealing with her own in terms of re-cycling and re-formation. Fermentation, a scientific process of maturing liquids and gases is able to help release nitrogen, oxygen, and certain essential gases that are crucial for human sustainability from decaying discarded tree parts—tree roots. Tree roots, a component of nature's bio-degraded agent is able to decompose its own into the soil as manure. These go to enrich the soil composition in the form of natural or organic fertilizers that in effect improves crop production and increase food security for human and animal sustenance. A greater percentage of these organic fertilizers in the soil will reduce the reliance on synthetic matter which is hazardous to the soil and humanity. Organic fertilizers are able to replace the lost soil nutrients that come as a result of over cultivation of a particular farmland.

Discarded tree roots in their decomposing stages become another source of food production. Mushrooms, worms, cocoon and caterpillars are hatched from these decomposing tree parts and become a source of human and animal protein. Worms and other insects that feed on certain plants and plant parts serves as animal virus on parasitic plants that may hamper crop production. These very worms and insects may also feed on certain disastrous

4

smaller insects and worms whose existence may further hamper crop production (Agriculture for Humanity). It is factual that some of these tree roots are processed for the production of medicine-based alcoholic and non-alcoholic beverages. Their chemical components are extracted through heat and chemical injection and added to the beverages at recommended quantity and dosage.

Despite the natural gains achieved from these discarded tree roots, their existence on the farmlands, residential backyards, industrial sites, constructional areas and institutional premises possesses as threat to humans and even animals. Naturally, they become the den for reptiles and other creeping animals and also convergence point for plastic waste, a non-degradable waste that has become difficult to contend with in Ghana and certain parts of Africa. Some huge discarded trees roots may possess certain deeper holes and groves which serve as canopy or resting place for lunatics and miscreants. These canopies may become possible spots for crime perpetuation since such may be congenial place for anti-social acts and behaviour.

The discovery and collection of tree roots as raw material for sculpture production may by itself serve as a mode of cleaning the environment as well as preventing them from becoming the collection point for fly-up and light weight non-degradable waste. They may therefore prevent contamination as a result of human contact, if not, then they become points for the breeding of mosquitoes and area noted for stings and bites by dangerous reptiles and other creeping animals. It is therefore essential for sculptors and nature artists to accept and take on some of these discarded tree roots as raw materials for art production.

## Treatment of Tree Roots

Identifying and fixing—collection, cleaning, pruning and pulling of luster as a technique may be recommended for the rendering of this nature art. The found and fixed products obtained from the discarded tree roots were thoroughly washed using the pressure pump. This was able to desilt and clean all the clay deposits clogged in the nook and cranny of the roots.

The washed pieces were allowed to dry thoroughly pending carving. The loose end weak parts and the unnecessary protrusions and projections were shortened or removed. The fixed pieces were immersed in a tank containing wood treatment solution for a period a week. The long immersion of artforms in the solution was to destroy all wood worms, termites, and insect that may affect the prolonged lives of these artforms. After the pieces were removed from the tank and put in the room temperature for gradual drying. A solution of sanding sealant with fluid viscosity was applied unto the pieces through the brush application technique. This was to seal all the wood pores on the surfaces of the roots just to improve upon the reception of the chemical finisher.

Upon thorough drying, a fine grade abrasive cloth was rubbed over the root surfaces from top to down and in all the nooks and cranny. The pieces were thoroughly dusted-off with a clean cloth and the vacuum pressure from the air compressor. The process was repeated to ensure that all the wood pores were sealed and the surface rendered fine and silky. These pieces were later finished with a fine wax pullover that offered them velvet wax finish. These selected tree roots and their success story have the ability to drive in or give hope to the hopeless in the community.

The following chapters—Chapter One: Champion, Chapter Two: Espouse, Chapter Three: Campaigner, Chapter Four: Pugilist, Chapter Five: Activist, offer the relationships that exist between the found and fixed tree roots that constitute these collection of thoughts and ideas of real life situations and happenings of people.

# CHAPTER ONE
# CHAMPION: ANCESTRAL DENIAL
## 'Awogyann'

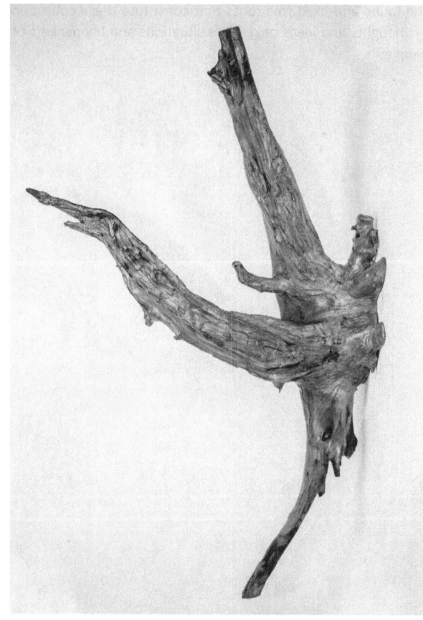

Plate One: Champion

'Champion' is a found root of an indigenous Ghanaian hard tree that has been fixed—cleaned, trimmed and varnished for interior and exterior decoration. The root has a compact base on which sits three major out stretched projections. These projections have smaller protrusions that spring from them. The middle projection is set in a vertical pose of twist and turn while the other two move in opposing direction that is to the left and right of the composition. The bark of the root structure has a bumpy texture that manifests the termites work on the root.

This makes the root to assume some tactile surface texture. The root has a natural ocher colour, a colour that portrays honour and wealth of royals. The root sculpture depicts the head mask of conqueror—a raised face and upper arms appearing from a pivot. It suggests the posture of a celebrating social hero. A person who has endured denial and rejection from his own but through the assistance of the cosmic world he has been able shoot into prominence.

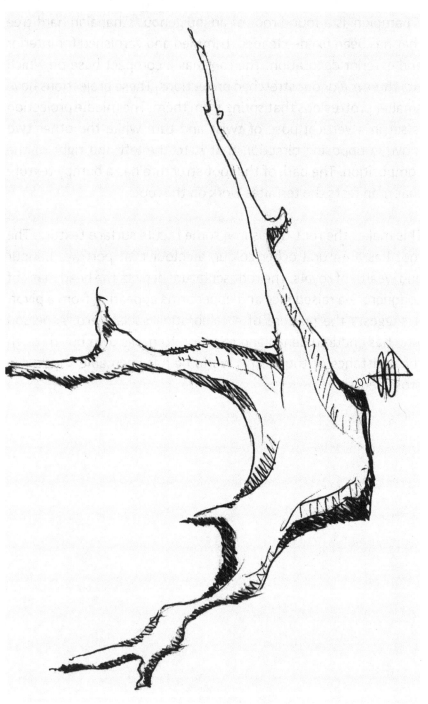

Figure One: Champion

There lived some time ago, a two-month old baby boy whose mother has bolted away and was just at the care of an ailing less-employed youth father. Hmmmm! as the story got unfolding, it came to the attention the community that, this baby boy was not the only off-spring (dependant) of this father but there were two additional siblings as well. The mother, an adolescent errand-girl and a migrant had thrown her hands in despair, given up her responsibilities and preferred restarting a new and better life elsewhere, a practice that has today become acceptable to Ghana's less-endowed youth.

The father, an alcoholic, an untrained cobbler, stationed at a popular lorry station and a market place in Agbogbloshie a densely populated community in the capital city and could only do with a merger proceed from his trade, a size of income which in Ghana is referred to as 'hand-to-mouth' income. Agbogbloshie, a populous suburb-environment where the hustle and bustle prevails for only the survivors, life trials are counted on daily basis. What you earn today takes you to the next day. There is the Ghanaian parlance that goes 'heaven helps those who help themselves', or in the popular Ghanaian highlife musician, Amakye Dede's rendition; se ekuro dosuaa wontsina fakor na wonngye enyenguase, meaning 'if you continuously sit in one spot you sit on your worth'. These indigenous clichés here mentioned propelled persons to be on the constant move just to meet the social pressures and dictates of human sustenance. These and other acts create neglect and abandonment within the Ghanaian society, something that leads to hopelessness among infants and the youth. Therefore, the less hearted will always off-load their burden unto others who are ready to bear.

In his admonishment to his followers, the celebrated speaker and preacher had inferred that any set-back is a set-up in the journey of success—Joel Osten. Mankind certainly possesses opaque lenses that prevent us from seeing afar in the realm of the unseen world. Donald Trump, the celebrated American's speech to the Americans on his perceptions on Africans and Arabs, insinuates that Africans refuse to see far, they only and always just perceive their immediate stretch of space, they do not see into the future and this eventually affect their development. In most situations, mankind is always limited by the cosmic perception of enabling us see that far. Being able to see into the future of persons is a scarce reality. We are definitely not able to anticipate the future associations, positions, and successes of people we rate low or disregard along the line of human relations.

Stunting one's prospects to life is a normal practice to witness. Therefore in an attempt to overturn the speculations and anticipations of observers, mankind usually abandons God's times and ways to make choices that are equated to the quick-fix and easy-fix syndromes, an option that usually leads us to return to the starting point or regret our earlier decisions. Inspirational and motivational speakers of both local and international stature, and the Akan culture have always reiterated that, 'say good things about yourself, or tell yourself you are the best, but quit remembering your negatives because they will eat you up at all times'. Just like the David story of the Bible days, in spite of all the set-backs of David, he always declared himself as the best and the best arrived at his doorstep.

In our modern day, child bearing has become one of the major challenges to several middle class couples. Today, several efforts are being made for people to become mothers and fathers as being one is certainly an honour to oneself, one's family and the society. To the African society, children are believed to be the reincarnation of the ancestors and that their appearance on the physical world provides joy, honour and continuity to the society. Several questions are being asked as to why and how orphanages are springing up everywhere and everyday in spite of the numerous challenges the elite class faces with child birth. Yet the lower class, the least educated and the less financially endowed continue to be the repositories of child itinerary, yet inability to bear the needs and wishes of these children. Is the African cosmic more benevolent to the marginalized rather than the economically, socially and academically upright persons? or Are they less sympathetic to the affluent rather than the less endowed? Maybe the affluent is not recognized enough or well sighted by the cosmic world. Or are they created to take care of the less endowed infants and orphans?

The question being asked in recent times is: Is the establishment of orphanages a quest to improve upon the plight of the unfortunate children? or Is it an attempt to enhance the financial stature of owners? or Is it to make marginalized children really happy? or Is it to put food on their table? or Is it to put shelter at their disposal? or Is it to offer them education?, or Is it to put clothes on them? or What? These are but the requirements of the Millennium Development Goals, a global policy that is enshrined to provide child development and safety by all nations and individuals. Yet in the African communities, child neglect and abandonment is pervasive and gradually becoming a canker. The teeming youth are turning in off-springs at their earlier ages, creating lot of teenage parents that are weary and unsupported. The elderly group or the aged parents are also giving birth at their later stages in life, creating what is known in Ghana as pension babies—children giving birth to at the blink of their parent retiring age from active employment. Even though the middle age group is touted as the sexually active and reproductive bracket, the political and economic policies of the nation has rendered majority highly unemployed and are therefore unable to take good care of their children as they may be expected.

Coupled with the social and cultural demands of the African society, the affluent and the poor are both expected to join in the race of providing the African ancestors the opportunity to reincarnate into the physical world and reconnect with the living. The baby boy in this context is one of such requirement, but he tries to adjust with the new world which is stained with poverty, filth and denial; in contrast with the spiritual world where his soul is connected with his creator and the benevolent spirits.

Growing up, the baby comes to appreciate the masculine single-parenting that confronts him. Mum is absent and mummy's siblings are un-reachable. Recuperating with health and a social matter was something that was unthinkable for the infant. Femininity was absolutely absent in the life of this infant. Singing of lullaby, cuddling, giggling, storytelling and others that offer babies soothing and gentle sleep mood had disappeared from the life of the infant. As the baby progresses to adjust to the father's new role, pediatric ailment sets in his life. Infection from the filthy environment and abode takes over and his health condition deteriorates.

The decline in the health status coupled with babysitting expose the poverty level of the ailing father, a condition that was very pathetic to contend with. Seeking a better medical assistance for the son has become rare for the father. Health insurance has not been subscribed for the family. The baby's soul though pure and strong has never encountered any standard medical facility. The closest Health and Medical Center to the infant's soul is the Over-the-Counter Licensed Chemical Shop, where the father contacted the seller, possibly, to procure a non-prescribed self-medicated pharmaceutical product for use.

Alternative medicine or the traditional medicine, a system that relies on herbs, tree trunks, barks and roots has been the most patronized medication by the indigenes and the less endowed in the community. These medications are found in every nook and cranny of the community. Though very popular to the community, their oral types are not recommended for infants. Possibly they are good for bathe and douse since their efficacy may be strong and dangerous to the throat and the intestines of the infant.

Seeking proper and intensive medical assistance and attention for infants is very essential for their growth and sustenance, since infants may not be able to express their health condition as adults do. It is therefore prudent for parents and guardians to acquaint themselves with the signs and symptoms that are associated with the common ailments of infants. Infants ailment require special knowledge and skills but there are limited accredited pediatrics and specialist medical facilities that have proven to be infant friendly and potent.

Such facilities are known and always recommended for prompt medical attention by family members, benevolent neighbours and good community members. Yet the less endowed holds the opinion that, though the pediatrics and specialist medical facilities services are prompt and efficient they are also very expensive to put up with and are therefore established for the privileged and the affluent in the society.

In African the community, the system allows for all members of the community to be responsive to each other's plight and condition in terms of guidance, direction and support for all persons and for the societal growth and survival. So, should the innocent soul of an infant be watched on to perish in the sight of the community while good and benevolent persons stay aloof? Why must the community be caught watching while fathers and mothers throw their hands in despair? Why must the community look on unconcerned to the deterioration of the precious gift from God and the ancestors? Oh no and never and never again. In situations where witches and wizards are caught causing havoc to their prey, traditional priests and priestesses are able to remedy situations by intervening to redeem the perishing from their predators. The community must not witness the death of this innocent soul.

There appears a benevolent community member, a neighbour in the market space, the place where the ailing father resides and operates his trade. The benevolent community member is someone who could not mind her own business as said in the Ghanaian phraseology. She exclaims 'how do I look on or see you destroy this precious baby's soul? I know of a nurse in the renowned state of the art government hospital who is kind and light hearted. The nurse will be able to help save the soul of this baby. Give the baby to me. If I spend the whole day in the hospital to save this soul and make no sale and profit from my stall, I will be blessed by the Almighty God for doing His work. This baby's soul is a precious one'. The benevolent neighbour takes on the duty of God to remedy the situation. The epoch has come for the baby to meet a better healthcare and parenting. The baby, wrapped in ragged and tatty apparels, is conveyed swiftly to the emergency ward of the renowned hospital.

The light hearted nurse takes over with the situation and leads the benevolent neighbour, the new guardian, to seek attention for the perishing infant soul. The infant is resuscitated but diagnosed of several infant related ailments: mal-nutrition, anemia, vitamin minuses, floppy muscle, and congenital and other hygiene induced infections. To resuscitate the infant, he needed to be in the intensive-care ward for some days as signs were good for his survival. In all this and as the day went by, the ailing father had not appeared but had prayed for the non-return of the baby since his presence has continuously added to his woe and predicament.

The later hours of the day saw the benevolent neighbour return without the baby and her sales for the previous day depleted. All her money had been spent on the health care of the infant.

The ailing father who had no hope and expectancy in the survival of child upon setting eyes on the neighbour then burst into tears, wailing and yelling, rolling and staggering: my son is gone, my son is dead, he has joined my fore-father and uncles, God take care of his soul for me, he's gone and he's gone to meet our ancestors. But as happy as he was, just to see his troubles go over in his staggering mood, the announcement came to him as a surprise, the son was alive and doing well, he has not given up the ghost, he is still with the living. What a cold bath, the poverty crises still prevail? Oh God! Why!? Even the death does not want the soul of the son. As said in Akan 'owu mpo mpeno' not even the death desires him.

Shame and guilt then clothe the ailing father as the community observers look onto his schematics and performances towards the presumed death of the child. Then he acclaims in style "foster him, take care of my son, take him forever, am no longer able to house, feed, clothe and also nurture him. I cannot be responsible for his needs and requirements, am not capable of fathering him in addition to the ones at home, take him or let the hospital own him forever, let him leave my sight and I donate him forever". The father now turns his back on the root of his future, the root that will be his bedrock. Like the Bible story; 'the stone the builder rejected shall become the head corner stone someday'.

The precious son, the holy infant and the darling boy becomes the sweet pie of the new guardian and hospital wardens. His rejuvenation in the days past offers some joy and pleasure to the guardian who now spends unending hours at the prestigious hospital ward. Watching the Baby darling kicking and rolling in his

17

cot with easy and ecstasy, delight and amusement gripped both the new guardian and the hospital staff. He attracted empathy and sympathy of the hospital staff and other parents who are there attending to their wards and those visiting their loved one at the hospital.

Day upon day, lots of gifts abounds his cot. These includes socks, layette, caps, dresses, blankets, toys, feeders, walkers, and others that comes in either as brand new or used booty. Medications and consumables did flow as and when the need arises. The darling boy now becomes a precious boy. His soiled surroundings now make way for the designer's ideal look and taste. The darling boy, now undeniably darling, wooed and continue to woo almost every sympathiser including the high and intermediary profiled medical gurus to himself. What an ancestral penetration and cosmic favour drawn to the infant? What an intervention! The once fed a day now has in-between meals; one dress a week now has a change over in regular intervals; the one without footwear and head protectors now has several of them for all season.

Darling boy has now gained weight and form, and his health status well improved to the admiration of the prestigious hospital staff. What an amazing record time of renaissance, a remarkable impression of health care and delivery to the almost a home call convict of an enormous rejection. He was a picturesque that had no intended connoisseur. Darling boy had to be discharged from the ward and the hospital for the simple reason that his health condition had improved remarkably and that fresh patients and newer convicts of death had arrived for same health care. A hospital bed must not be a permanent abode to persons. It is a health transitory space meant for the weak, ailing souls or persons.

Medical bills and consultancy fees to be paid took over the joy the boy has managed to experience in relation to his well-being. How does he get out of the hospital without settling the accrued bills? Who takes care of these bills to enable the easy exit and reunion of the infant with the family or the guardian? Where does he go from the hospital since the ailing father has literally donated him to the guardian and the hospital? Must the hospital absorb the bills as bad debt and have possession of him as well? Maybe the hospital will nurture and allow him to work as a labourer to pay-off or settle his debt in future as an adult captive? Does the hospital know the ailing father? Did the father know the hospital where the son was admitted into? Did the father visit the son while in the hospital? Perhaps he could have attracted some attention and sympathy from the medical facility just as the son did.

Does the Almighty God work through man or does He work through saints and angels. Presumably, like what has been taking place in the urban center in developing countries, discharged patients are quarantined in the hospital or kept in the confinement of the ward until their bills are fully honoured, else they bolt away without settling the bills. Will that be the case of the darling boy?

Your guess may be as good as mine. Where will a philanthropist come from as onlookers wait on to see the actions and decisions of the hospital authorities? Situations like this have occurred elsewhere when the hospital authorities wrote-off the discharged patients bill and declared it as bad debt. Should the hospital be declaring several of these bills as bad debt, what then will be left for the running and maintenance as well as re stocking of the facility? As this went on, the darling boy kept enjoying his stay in the posh hospital figuring out when the father and the guardian or the health philanthropist would rescue him from his plight. Parents of other patients draw closer to infer among each other so as to know if there is the need to make silver collection or contributions to settle the surmounting bills of the darling boy, but no finale could be drawn since not all persons have the spirit of giving or supporting one another. As though that may not be conclusive, the health philanthropist then moves to the closet to take guidance and directions from the Almighty God.

Meanwhile, the benevolent neighbour and guardian just joined the ailing father in throwing her arms into the air because all her capital have diminished and her customers have dwindled, she bolted from the confines of the hospital, unknowingly, to abandon the glory of the Lord that was to come upon her. Since mankind is unable to anticipate the future of their children, there is always the possibility of turning ones back on them instead of continuing the golden or silver hand we extend to the needy. 'Doing it for children means doing it for the Lord'.

The health philanthropist then comes from the closet after a serious discerning thought to announce her willingness to take up cost involved and pay the medical bills of the darling boy. Although, she was not capable or in position to offset the total cost of the almost a month stay in the hospital by the infant, the hospital had modalities laid for staff to enjoy some financial waiver and also a flexible payment pattern for medical bills accrued by staff.

The health philanthropist then pronounces the intention and concludes the payment pattern with the hospital authorities to offer the infant the opportunity to reunite with the family. This kind gesture beams the face of the darling boy with delightful joy. He then smiles, laughs and giggles to the medical staffs in a manner that goes to express his appreciation to the Almighty God and mankind, an appreciation, that opens up prospects for future favours and blessings. The Africa community teaches it own to offer appreciation for all favours that comes their way.

The health philanthropist presents the documents for the discharge of the darling boy and that sets the darling boy on the way to the family for a resounding reunion. A reunion with whom? When? and where? The exit from the hospital comes with another phase of abandonment and silent negotiation. The benevolent neighbour, the person who ushered the darling boy into the prestigious hospital never comes into sight again in the hospital to take the infant back to the ailing father.

Perhaps she is seen to be in a similar predicament as the ailing father. She lacks the decent accommodation to host the boy for a long stay since the ailing father has no interest in having the boy again. Perhaps as a Spinster and unattached female she may have thought the attachment of the darling boy would technically deter bachelors and unattached men from getting attracted to her.

The day has again gone by, the health philanthropist has ended the service for the day and still the benevolent neighbour has still not arrived at the hospital to convey the darling boy home. Since the bed has been allocated to another infant, there was the need for him to vacate the bed for the new patient. Based on this, the health philanthropist has to assume the position of the new guardian and therefore decided to allow the darling boy to pass the night, at least, at her residence and send him back to the hospital the next day in case the father or the guardian does come for him.

The darling boy now appears in the hospital, the work place but now in the changing and resting bar for the staff, a practice that is permissible for nursing mothers who are on duty. The process of conveying the baby to and from the hospital has become another responsibility of the health philanthropist. She has a new baby to contend with. As a spinster and a distant attached person, she has to go through the new ordeal of awakening, bathing and cuddling the darling boy as part of her day and night responsibility.

In the attempt to pursue nature and God's service to mankind, the continuous attention and care had to be given to the darling boy. In all this, friends, colleagues of the hospital and health philanthropist pursued the search to locate the benevolent neighbour and the father of the darling boy in the neighbourhood of their address. How can one locate person(s) in a community without proper house address and identity? The search pervades unending for over a week and finally both the benevolent and the ailing father are identified and summoned for the takeover of their responsibility. In all these, the health philanthropist and her associate had evolved and bonded together with the darling boy with so much love.

A sense of belongingness and attraction had been established. The darling boy had consumed his caretakers into becoming the rightful guardians. A social media WhatsApp message that went trending indicated that: 'when faced with challenges, do not run away, fix them, learn from them and understand what you need to do, so that you never repeat them. The richest wealth is wisdom but the strongest weapon is courage'.

The health philanthropist and her associates had persuaded the father and the guardian to pick the boy but to no avail. The father and the guardian returned the persuasion to the neglect of the boy since his presence in their community was just as good as allowing the boy come back to his previous health status. He was going to be raised in a very dysfunctional environment and that newly gain health and social stature was going to deplete him back to the level which had gotten him to the hospital.

In all these, the ancestors of the darling boy were working exceedingly in the cosmic world to reposition him into a privileged family and wealthy home. Like the Bible story, 'child Moses' status and the mother's ploy to get the child Moses received into the king's palace, God and the cosmic world had prepared a better place and a palace for the boy—a good environment, good education, good upbringing and a brighter future, a favour that qualified him to a more than a double dose of God's favour. He therefore gains family membership status rather than a simple adoption.

Discussions have been concluded and it has been agreed that the darling boy should keep on staying with the health philanthropist and her associates so he can complete his medication and enjoy a refreshed life pattern. Upon a period of 'to and fro' thus: home-work-home, and the improved health rejuvenation, the darling boy was transfer to an associate, an elite, a sister of the royal family who is a senior health practitioner for an enhanced conditioning pending a further transfer to the real royal home of the health philanthropist. Darling boy is privileged to stay and mingle with the elites of the senior health practitioner as an intermediary preparation to the royal destination. A destination that is honourable and respectful.

Training and mentoring of a non-royal infant into the royal confines is a matter of great concerns. Royals are offered the opportunity to act and behave as elites in the community. The mannerisms, the customs, the traditions, the norms and the beliefs of the community reside in the elites. Elites are the custodians or the repositories of the traditions. Therefore ways to speak, greet, walk, dress, dance, and eat and others are well measured and tailored towards the expectation of the community. As an infant and an inducted royal, meeting the expectation of the royals was something that could not be fathomed, but what do you do? Just comply with the wishes of the elites, after all, becoming a royal was the new order.

Couples of months have gone by and just as the mentoring and nurturing proceeded, the infant had to make a triumphant entry into the royal home. The long expected member, the young elite, a quasi-heir to the throne, an Ɔdehye had arrived into the Addo Royal Family through Princess Naa Addobea, the princess of the Pillow Chief—Sundzehene. A grand naming ceremony and an outdooring are organized for him and the royal title Nana Addo Kwebi is conferred on him. He is named after the grandfather.

The darling boy – the half-year-old grand prince proceeds with the further nurturing and mentoring to become a full fledge elite of the community. Elites near and far, inside and outside the country and friends of the throne had been briefed of the entry of the new prince.

This catches the attention of elites and friends of near and far to furnish the prince with cloths, goodies, and pleasantries. He is enlisted in one of the best schools which all the elites of the Addo Royal Family attend. He is also taken through the necessary sports, music, dances and humour lessons and skills to enhance his physique, psyche and appearance orientation as all the elites are made to go through. This was also to quash the trace of his genetic and take on the new royal ambiance. The darling boy grows into adolescence and becomes a young adult of an adorable stature, psyche, appearance and full of hospitable culture.

As he takes his brilliance from the secondary to the tertiary educational cycle where he pursues higher degree in hospitality and tourism management, a trade he grew up into. His environment was full of hospitality establishment and as royals, touring was their priority. His sporting prowess and enthusiasm won him bursary and scholarship as a basket ball player and an athlete. As a sport enthusiast, he had all the support from the family. He had access to several sporting facilities at home which included basket ball court, tennis court and running tracks. In addition, he had training manuals and video sent to him from relations abroad.

The home had satellite and internet connectivity to access world class basket ball and athletics' clubs for grooming. He also had the services of personal coaches who were engaged for his sporting talent and career right from the childhood. These and other support schemes made him an outstanding sportsman, disciplined and sharp to attract foreign clubs and universities. Darling royal, Nana Addo Kwebi now graduates from a highly rated university with Masters Degree in Hospitality and Tourism Management, returns to his home land Ghana, and establishes hospitality facilities with his foreign partners in Akwapim and Accra the capital city. He also establishes a sports academy to harness talent for his foreign clubs and Ghana.

Looking back to the days of his rejection by the biological parents, what would have been the fate of Nana Addo Kwebi, if the ailing father had prevented the neighbour from pursuing orthodox medicine for him or what would have been the fate if the prestigious hospital had refused him the medical attention due to his sorry appearance?, or what would have been the fate if the hospital philanthropist and princess Naa Addo had not accepted to adopt him into the royal home? or what would have been the faith if Nana Kwebi, the Sundzehene of the Addo palace had not welcomed him, offered royal status and extended royalty or chiefdom courtesies to him?

Like the preacher—Joel Osten said 'Take God First and He Will Take You To Places You Never Dreamt Of' the humility, love for all persons and compassion for the elderly and the poor and the good religious principles that were instilled in him brought him to the understanding and level that could never be imagined. Good family, good association and good community systems allow the survival and the growth of all persons and the community as well. The physical world is limited by what is shrouded in the future. Men are limited by sight and therefore are unable to perceive accurately, it is only the cosmic world that has some revelations to the future of people. Let us keep our own and nurture them for tomorrow, let us negotiate for the best if we are unable to make it work for us for all humans are the best treasures of the world. Welcome home and to the Akanland of Nana Addo Kwebi.

The 'Champion' root educates us on the lesson that when a person who has endured denial and rejection from his generation— parents, relations and community but comes to terms with the assistance of the cosmic world, she or he will be able move into prominence through the grace of the Almighty God the creator.

# CHAPTER TWO
## ESPOUSE: OCCUPATIONAL ROMANCE
### 'Ajumakromu Ɔdɔ'

Plate Two: Espouse

'Espouse' is a found Acacia Root that has been fixed— cleaned, trimmed and varnished for interior and exterior decoration. The acacia root has been rendered in its natural and burnt umber colour combination a scheme that has the propensity to cover dirt and filth. The acacia root professes flamboyant compact structure of several root stock heads that emanate from a curly s-shape base.

The base has a smooth and firm structure on which the uncontrolled root that offers that type of dynamism sits on. The compact movement from root head depicts stalagmite/ stalactite-like structures that suggest growth in relationship. These render support to each other in an attempt to provide some type of occupational efficiency, advocacy, recreation and pleasure.

**Figure Two: Espouse**

In a morning devotion session, the leader mentioned that 'God loves us all, but He has favourites too'. This saying impressed and inspired the members of the group that it was further talked about among families in the community. At a family gathering, the head of the maternal alluded that "the value the Almighty God has situated in a fetus leading to child birth—human being is so permanent that no single individual can change or lower the esteem, looks and destiny of the favoured.

He concluded that, persons under certain paternal utterances and pressures must not allow themselves to be eluded by such petty paternal judgment that has the tendency to impact on their internal, external and expected personal life qualities negatively. People are simply gifts from God and that God gifts are undeniable, no man can put away God's gifts. The family elder further mentioned that Africans children are presumed to be the re-incarnated ancestors, therefore pregnancy is deem as the process of starting the transfiguration of the spiritual into the physical world.

In a feminine fashion towards courtship, the practice has always been that, male superiors in organization are normally admired and attracted to by female subordinates. As the cliché goes 'females aspire for males of higher ranks to date or enter into serious relationship with and marry'. This perceived standard practice pursued by most females creates some form of discomfort for higher ranked females who as a matter of their higher academic and professional attainment have to accept proposals from males below their cadre. It is quite intriguing to observe that, higher ranked females who are attached to higher ranked males or men of same status are fewer. In fact, every organization has fewer higher ranking officials. It is revealing that fewer higher ranked females find it comfortable to be in relationship men far below their status. Therefore higher ranked females who attempt to be in love with lower ranked males are seriously mocked by the society. For that reason, the wider the gap that exists between a higher ranked female and a lower ranked male, the greater the discomfort of choices and impossibilities of relationship and marriage. A wider status gap between top brass females and low brass males makes it difficult for the higher ranked females to showcase or exhibit their lower ranked spouses among their peers.

In a similar fashion, the same cliché has been established for the averaged height and the vertically-challenged females to prefer, fall for or possible accept proposals for dating, enhancement relationship and also marriage from tall and taller males even when such men are baggage with numerous challenges. In a relationship discussion on a local radio station in Takoradi, a panelist inferred that 'aspiring wives and female lovers prefer looking up when charting with their male counterparts than they fixing their heads downwards towards the faces of the males'. Among the Akans, the idiom from females has been 'who raises the head in a communication pattern - female or male?' The standard practice has been for the female to raise the head to meet the lowering face of the male most especially in the process of caressing and emotional (kisses) exchanges.

Males are naturally framed to be taller and stronger than females. The masculine frame of males offers the female the confidence, security and surety especially when couples are in the public space. The sociological belief of verticality (height) and structural (upright figure) respect bestowed unto males give the impression of being superior over females. Mockery is therefore usually made of females who have been blessed by God to be tall and also super-structured like or more than their male counterparts as compared to the averaged or less of the female stock.

The question has always been that, these above average structured females, who they should turn to for spousal choices: very tall, excessively tall and excessively structure males or male of their equal height and size or less. An interaction with Miss 'A' (a very tall and very structured female) with respect to her spousal or dating choices revealed that over seventy percent of the males who reach out to her for date are those of the average male body size and height or lower. So I asked, what may be the reason for your attraction to these light body and vertically-challenged men. Miss 'A' reiterated that possibly such challenged males are may be interested in having a blend of children bigger and taller than their body frame and image.

Probable, as cute as these males may look, they also attempt to seek prominence through such tall and well framed females. Or it could also be an attempt to compensate their God giving body size for that of the super framed females. Miss 'A' concluded that several well-structured and tall females desire their contemporary male sizes but they a few are able to achieve that desire, possibly men of their sizes also attracts the cute females. A notable example is the well educated females who do not usually have their preferred choices of males. Very few highly educated females are able to attract the highly educated males. They are equally mocked for a reverse of the normality. Yet the good Lord admonishes them to maintain their self acceptance culture.

In another like situation, females who are or have become financially endowed are also seen in a similar situation like the well educated and the well structured females. Being a female and a well-resourced or financially endowed also equally stretches the standard cliché of females 'looking up' to the male counterpart for financial support at all times. In the recent past and even today, many females look up to dating proposals from the financially endowed males. In fact, several low income females are quick to run into the arms of these male-financial don irrespective of their looks, education and character.

The practice has been that, the males are and must be the natural bread winners of homes and families. The good book, Bible story position males as the one created to toil and to provide food and shelter and security for their wives and children. Males are expected to provide for their wives and children food, clothe, shelter and education. These natural responsibility ordained unto males has invariably coded numerous females from pursuing their God giving gifts and talent of being the repositories of worth and wealth. The females have depended totally on their males for support and goodies.

The fact still remains that, in most African homes today, females are the ones who control the finances. Female are now in many professions and trades that hitherto were the preserve of males. Career women in Africa are the ones providing meals, homes, clothes, education and health care for children, family and fiancées. At times, they work hard to procure accommodation, vehicle and home for their families. The issue of single-parenting has unveiled this very twist to social and economic empowering of the females. In today's Africa, more females are being educated, resourced and projected just as or even more than their male counterparts. Everything that men do women can do and do them better.

In this masculine world of ours, females are declared potentials subordinate to the human race. The truth is that one's self worth does not come from what people think and perceive of us, rather, the true sense of self worth is what has been created in us by the Almighty God and Creator. Ones looks talents, worth, values are gifts from God accept them and make the best of life's journey. We are God's Masterpiece (Ephesians 2:10). The question is what is a Masterpiece? A masterpiece is an authentic copy, uniquely created pieces. It is not a carbon copy or a mass produced piece. If an artist can create a masterpiece that is of a unique value and has the ability to withstand the test of time, then why not the human being who is the creation of the Almighty God.

Occupational romance has been that sour type of relationship that has it trace more often than not much uncovered. In simple term, it is that relationship resulting from workplace romance. This relationship has its roots stretching beyond expectation. It is imaginable and quite consuming. One may ask the question, what may be the reason beneath this type of romance? Could it be for equalization of task and human resources delivery, complement of higher performance, labour fusion or agape love? Perhaps, several work persons are enrolled into this relationship making it extremely impossible to perceive its success or otherwise its fruits or pains.

So what then is occupational romance? Occupation may be defined as the activity in which one is engaged, or the principal business of one's life, a vocation, the holding of an office or position — (The Mirror, June 2016) Romance may be defined as an emotional attraction, a passionate love affair, to carry on a love affair between two persons, and in this case a male and a female. Therefore, one may say that, occupational romance is that type of romantic thoughts and ideas, or amorous relationship relating to or resulting from a particular occupation that exit between opposite sex of the same trade or skills, of different trade or skill, of the same rank or different rank, of the same department or different department within the same institution or establishment.

In recent times, persons employed in same institutions happen to find their love companions among their work force. Seeking for love companions has become a major challenge for the youth of Africa. Occupational romance starts in the form of utterances, which are uttering compliments to colleagues, subordinates and superiors. Showing compliments to persons in a work place has been seen as a major work performance drive to colleagues and customers. Showing compliment to persons and colleagues sometimes leads to flirting among these persons.

Flirting is an act that makes people to behave amorously without serious intents towards one another. Flirting has no initial amorous intent, yet may leads to something that may be unimaginable. In many work places and other organizations, several persons flirt through the use of words, eye contacts, body language and touch. Though such means of communication may be appreciated in harmless responses, their continuous echoing to spinsters and bachelors may send some deep feeling of erotic language to the recipients.

Previously, in the Akan culture, persons looking for love companions and potential spouses had to go through the family trail. Family leaders led the search for better life partners for their wards. Akan males had to wait for either their paternal or maternal uncles or other family leaders to search and recommend appropriate and commendable wives for them as future wives. Females who were potential wives needed to meet certain demonstrable marriage criteria. Family order and status were crucial when selecting females as possible wives.

Wives were selected from families who professed virtue, resourcefulness, service, servitude and honour. Wives were found from among the best of the ethnicity, family and females. Females who take it upon themselves to search for better halves or love companions always suffer the consequence thereof. So what is the standard order for seeking for a male love companion or an aspiring husband?

In the past, male partners or male prospectors and aspiring husbands had to demonstrate bravery, strength, wisdom, responsiveness, and quality leadership. Males had to be raised by families that had clean records that were free from pilfering, adulterous, contagious sickness, laziness, bad temper, among others. In today's Africa, the male youth have taken it upon themselves the responsibility to search for their own life partners. Love is invariably found and practiced in every corner of the community—night clubs, bars, spot, schools, workplace, coaches, social centers, just to mention a few. Lovers meet to express and consume love at all times.

Today, some African female youth have the pungent for premarital relationship and therefore are quick to introduce their lovers to the parents for their acceptance. This is something that is contrarily to the African and Akan customary marriage practice of waiting to be married through recommendation by family members. Negative and unpleasant consequential situations that elude most of these urbanized relations often lead to their traumatic termination. They usually leave behind traces of regret, disappointment, denial, rejection and possibly dependencies that they do not hope to contain.

In his usual psychedelic inspirational presentation, the renowned preacher Joel Osten admonishes his audience that 'people are not always who they say they are but if you rely on God's wisdom and knowledge—messages, you will find out what people really are'. A beautiful relationship between a young male and young female medical professional just got cozy and rosy. Cushy love, a selected principle and element of belonging had buzzed the environment of these youth professionals. Fraternity and togetherness had clouded them. Caressing and sharing of love had peaked beyond measure, as if they were in a different world, an ecstasy that existed for them alone. As the saying goes 'everybody needed somebody'. At this instance the lovers needed each other the most. As the saying goes, 'a man with a focus never flops'. Making a target to win a lover is a must for the males. The need for a lover at that moment was the matter of fact.

As medical persons, the act of caring, sharing and maintenance of in-patient and out-patient had fast embraced their love too. The sweet love environment had fast drowned their love to the extreme angle of their amorous and trying out relationship. Gifts and pleasantries had swung to each other especially towards their guardians and family members. Love felicitations were so warm that nothing could stand between these passionate health lovers. It was as if the oath of service pronounced by these health professionals had been extended to their love audition. It has been said that 'do not ride over what your feeling expresses. Let the discerning spirit of the Lord lead you to the real destination.

Health practitioners at all levels perceive the unflinching love that is bound to exist between them and their patients. It is very apt to see how young female nurses/ health staffs attached their practice of service and survival to their out-patients and especially in-patients, a service that is offered without noticing the unpleasant, eye sore and filth associated with it. Bathing, feeding, administration of medication, emptying of bed pans, urine pots, sweat bags and occasional errands at the health facilities are done with rapt attention. These and other duties that are enjoyed by in-patients are in some situations extended to out-patients who are domicile—domiciling health service. All these traditional services of the female nurse or health staffs are extended to their loved ones.

Another service offered by akin health practitioner—pharmacist has been in the area of drug consultancy, preparation and dispensing. This appendage of the health professionals has the responsibility to recommend the appropriate medication, ingredients, composition and dosage to their patient's recovery. As a health professional, alleviating sufferings and ensuring comfort of the clients is the priority. Nurses and pharmacists have a common love for their patients and clients hence their attraction for each other.

Oh love! What is love? What is the meaning of love to the youth of Africa? Love is like a found piece of raw gold. It needs to be processed and polished to make it attractive to its observers. Like the jeweler, the art of processing a gold piece is done with utmost skill and care. Love if found must be processed to the admiration of its partner. Lovers do their best to gain attention from the loved and as well to ensure the final tying of the knot at the family altar. Relationship when not properly consumed leads to pregnancies that are unexpected.

Pregnancy at an early stage of the relationship may not guaranty the continuous pleasantries of a wavy love. You have been chosen by the Almighty God. You have been had picked by the Almighty God (1st Peter 2:9). Dr. Mensa Otabil, the celebrated Ghanaian preacher infers that 'the value that the Almighty God put in His children is permanent. And that no person(s) can change or lower the destiny, looks and opportunities bestowed in a person, therefore one must not allow peoples judgments to affect the internal qualities that God has put in him or her.' This motivational exposition has been seen as a wide shield that provides a continuous assurance to a life fulfilling journey to the rejected and the dejected.

These wise words offers inspirations to persons affected in a way, and therefore brings them to terms that, they should rather turn to the Almighty God for solutions instead of depending on their personal strength and allowing their problems to devour them up. People must be chosen royals. When the Almighty God chooses you nothing will be able to stop your success. People may reject you but God will surely accept you if you make Him your first choice. God pays His labourers much better than that of man. God extends the movement of the chosen further than what they can anticipate. When God steps into ones ways, His abilities are discovered, enhanced and perfected to the amusement of all human kind.

Here comes the notice of the pregnancy, a result of the sweet pleasure of the lovers. The young female heath professional has taken a seed out of the relationship that she had started with the male co-worker. Occupational romance at its best! Joy had set in the heart of the female health practitioner. This joy is at the instance of the fetus reaction of the new soul about to manifest as into another human being—a creation of God, an expected ancestor to be reincarnated. The seed of the great one has germinated and natured. The seed marks the beginning of that great speaker, great professional, great inspirer, great planner, great designer, great master-hand that is about to be born, out-doored and named.

## Pregnancy
Pregnancy, according to the African and Akan philosophy marks the start of the process of reincarnation. Pregnancy is the process where an ancestor returns to the physical world to continue with the work of the Creator. According to the African, pregnancy is a mystery. The period that the Unseen decides to be Seen. Ancestors start the process of becoming humans. Pregnancy is not questioned at its instance since any unpleasant utterance

may be a disregard of the Almighty God and the ancestor who has volunteered to honour the couple or will be couple or their family.

The Akans belief that a pregnant person must be made to go through the full term of the pregnancy and deliver before marriage is scheduled and performed. Therefore any contention about a pregnancy ought to be postponed until the child is born. Then the truth may be ascertained either by resemblance or through clinical procedures.

Celebrating motherhood is very crucial to the African and the Akans. Therefore females result to all ways and means to become pregnant. Like the Bible story surrounding the pregnancy and birth of these greatest preachers and redeemers— John the Baptist, Jesus Christ and Samuel. In all these circumstances, the females and mothers of these great leaders express the feeling of joy and disbelief at the instance of the alertness of the pregnancy. Therefore, celebrating another great soul, an African germ, carried by a virgin, to an African health practitioner was fairly news to hear.

Pronouncing the pregnancy to the aspiring husband took the form of the contemplation of the annunciation of the pregnancy of Jesus to Joseph by the Virgin Mary. Unlike in the case of Virgin Mary where the Holy Spirit had to perform the annunciation, that of men requires some tactfulness and special verbal and non-verbal communication skill, since the announcement could be met with joy or tension, acceptance or rejection, dejection or deception and many others.

To the African, a denial, a refusal or a rejection of any particular pregnancy by a male (aspiring husband) bring unto the family of the female disgrace, shame and embarrassment. Therefore an acceptance of any pregnancy by a male (aspiring husband) bring unto the female's family honour, relief and joy. The community will accord the would-be couple some respect and dignity. An invitation to the male health practitioner, the aspiring husband to meet with the family of the female health practitioner, the expectant mother, had a show of ego, pride, remorseless and compassionless.

A clash of elitism, restrictedness and superiority eludes the perceived peaceful meeting expected to maintain and welcome the expected ancestor. A grand welcome ceremony, a love feast was through at the instance of the aspiring husband. This party was marred as the guest smells out suspicion and uttered his innocence to the pregnancy. The male (aspiring husband) got away from his suspense, guilt and articulated his non-acceptance of the pregnancy. This brought some form of straight face to the other colleagues and the cousins that were in his company.

This relationship has been well publicized and that some friends and colleagues of the aspiring husband or male lover had approved and concerted to their love trails. So this chauvinist attitude and aptitude comes as a surprise to these friends and family of the aspirant. He is hauled to the side and talked to offer a second thought to his resentment at the announcement of the taking of the seed by the colleague lover. Like the usual masculinity practiced by several male bosses, he later demonstrates some degree of acceptance of the purported pregnancy since he has remembrance of some amorous acts with the colleague and therefore pledges to offer some occasional remittances to the mother and child only when the baby is born and has resemblance of him, an act that has become a practice and the pride of some elite and affluent Africans male who take undue advantage of their social and financial status to cause havoc to innocent young ladies and pay their way and shame in a latter period when most of the pain and duty cost has been borne by others.

## Birth

The period of pregnancy and child birth in this relationship was clouded with pain, sorrow and feeling of rejection and denial. As the expectant mother goes through the period of body transformation and pain, the lover, the male co-worker rather shows very little care and love to the child and the mother. Thank God the political system allows for the policy of free maternal and free delivery for all women irrespective of your social and family stature. The day of the delivery of the child has come and the male co-worker is informed and called upon to assist in the process of delivery and the provision of medication for induced-labour, medically aided instruments and gadget and possibly intervene in talking to his superior medical colleagues to assist in getting the child delivered.

Yet, he shows no compassion to the situation and stands aloof as complication sets in as the labouring mother is seen passing on. Finally, the mother goes through the delivered and the baby is born. The delivery is through the breech method under the assistance of Obstetrician, a specialist who is sympathetic to females. Females who have been psychologically and traumatically mishandled by males and especially male superiors carry their pain and guilt forever. The Akan culture cherishes the process of child bearing and therefore honours females who are able to go through child delivery successfully. Children are said to be blessing from God. A female who is unable to make the process and therefore loses her life or that of the child is seen as being admonished and punished by the deities and Unseen spirits.

Therefore successful female-mothers are celebrated and offered the best of courtesy, goodies and honour. Fowl, sheep or cow is slaughtered on behalf of the female-mother as way of offering gratitude to the Almighty God, deities, ancestors and benevolent spirits for seeing their own through the battle of child bearing and also allowing an ancestor to come back to the physical world. The choice of animal for slaughter is dependent on the husband and the family's financial standing and level of gratitude. In this instance, the male colleague, the aspiring husband, the wife abandoner, absentee aspiring husband is absent and unavailable to provide an animal for this purpose in spite of the fact that the new born child, the first male child who may be the heir, is a true replica of the male health colleague and father.

The news then goes wild, like a bush-fire in the health facility and workplace. The contentious son, the new born, has the exact looks of the father. The deeds of the father have been exposed. There is no secret in this world that will forever be hidden. It is only the Almighty God that can reveal and uncover the deeds of mankind. Therefore, any attempt to with hold or keep the secret of man from God will not prevail. Man proposes but God dispose. The mother and child survive the ordeal of birth and transformation. Once the child birth and ancestral transfiguration have been completed, the mother and child are discharged from the health facility to their maternal home.

Mother and child appeared in the workplace, the health facility for post natal check up and medical consultation. Mother becomes fit and strong to resume for official duties as the baby boy grows well, healthy and bouncy. In all these, the father, the male colleague and the father who refuses to honour his responsibility of out-dooring and naming of the now look alike baby. Months upon mouths and days after days, the needed remittances for the upkeep of the baby have rather been silenced not to mention the occasion pattern that was echoed. For the period in question the official naming and out-dooring ceremony has not been honour and performed by the either the male colleague or his family.

His cross-cultural and migrant employment does exist as part of national integration and unity; it is always possible to have persons to seek employment in (a) community where little or no trace could be made of their family tiers or background. The possibility of having certain persons being officially married to persons who may not have the opportunity to accompany spouses or also relocate due to some official duties, lack of employment or trade, or, maybe, due to lack of interest in the new working terrain of the partner may cause some persons to veer into some extra marital and amorous relationship without the intention of ceiling it up with either marriage or prolonged relationship.

This sometimes led to unplanned child birth, something that may create a dislike and disaffection for both the mother and child or the mother or the child. This may lead to an act of shunning one's own parental and financial responsibilities towards a mother and a child or both.

As members of the Catholic fraternity, where naming and baptismal ceremony had to be performed for infants, the God Parents had to step in to as the father to perform such role in the church. Out-dooring ceremony that has not been sanctioned by the father had already been ushered by the mother's family to pave way for the naming ceremony in the church. In all these circumstances, although the surname of the father had been put on the baby, the Godfather and the Papacy had to provide a befitting the first and Christian name for the baby. This was to make him a true faith of the Catholic fraternity.

The father, the male colleague's refusal to touch and hold the baby presented to him to signify fatherly bond, blessing and love that were to connect the father to son and also offer a spiritual cover expected of the father according to the Akan culture. Grieve; pain, hurt, bitterness and unforgiving mood had now become the inner companion of the mother and colleague. Emotions and challenges—long suffering, shame and confusion blurs the love and affection that was envisaged and presumed.

Yet the feelings of guilt and pain for vengeance were calmed down through the prayer and words of the Almighty God and the good book. There is the Akan adage that if a spouse abandons his or her responsibility unto the other, the good God we have will clothe the neglected with the strength and blessing of the abandoner' that is how come some fathers, though are able to make several wealth and financial gains, may grow poorer and weaker in their later days as they wait and watch their abandoned and neglected become prosperous for them to go begging at their feet.

**Educating and Raising the Child**
Raising and educating children in Ghana and some parts of Africa is the responsibility of males—fathers. The Akan physiological philosophy puts the father as the one who provides the spiritual cover to the child. There is the Akan saying that 'Egya ne sunsum na okata nemba do' meaning 'the father spirit provides the well being of children.' Although, the Akans also believe that 'Ena ne mbogyataw na oye ba' meaning 'it is the blood of the mother that provides the blood of the child.' The Akans also demonstrate the understanding that the Almighty God is the one that creates the human being therefore the soul of the child comes from Him alone.

Inspite of these, the Akans still sees the fathers' contribution as crucial to the raising and educating of children. The Akan philosophy puts the father first in all the lines of responsibility, making the father the sole provider of the needs and wants of the family which includes that of infants and children. Therefore, a shirking of this responsibility is deemed irresponsible.

Persons of the Akan culture are known to be passionate in their practice of the matrilineal kind of inheritance which makes children born to Akan parents to belong to their maternal family tree. This is one kind of African culture that allows mothers to possess and showcase children from their marriage as part of their family possession and wealth. Hence the Akan adage 'sɛ *besia kɔ awarea ɔdzepa ba fie*' meaning 'a married woman bring wealth and fame to her family and lineage.' This is as result of the quality of child or children she is able to raise.

As though this is not enough, mothers have the natural responsibility of cradling infants and children from the embryo till their adolescent state. Mothers have the natural responsibility for nurturing infants and children for the betterment of the family, community and society. Since Akan children are the natural property of their mother's families, raising Akan children is seen as a sole duty and a shared responsibility of the couples.

Paternal control and responsibility towards children are crucial to the formation and development of the youth. Fathers, notwithstanding their Akan inheritance and inclination have the responsibility to ensure a sturdy emotional, social and academic wellbeing of their children. The Akan culture believes that since children do not work to earn income, their upkeep and economic responsibility lies squarely on those who bring them into the world. Incomes accrued by parents especially fathers must be properly scheduled to also include stipend for the raising of their children. Non performance of such responsibility could be labeled as a shirked responsibility.

## Academic Performance and Progression
Schooling and academic performance and progression is one bit that brings joy and pride to parents and guardians as their infants and dependants hit the classroom. In the Ghanaian labour terrain,

46

career women who have to resume for work after maternity leave have the legal backing to start work an hour later and end an hour earlier than their colleagues in the same establishment. This therefore makes it possible and easy for parents to drop and pick children to and from pre-school. Schooling to some kids becomes pretty intriguing when they are dropped and picked by their parents or especially the fathers particularly when kids are able to impress on their dads/fathers to buy them candies and toys at the least of request than the mums.

Days and years of the pre-school have passed so quickly and Junior (the darling boy) had moved onto the later sessions of the basic education. Lessons on life skills, vocational skills, science and mathematics as well as grammar had gone well with him. Academically he could be placed among the second ten of a class of hundred. Talent, ingenuity and intuition had permeated his schooling and formation. Companionship, compassion, responsiveness receptiveness, and openness have become the hallmark of Junior. Both instructors and candidates of the community school that Junior attends have a great testimony to his apt and adorable composure and stature.

Growing up, Junior has taken the physical type and look of the father, an appearance that makes it easy for persons to identify him with the father. As a son of health professionals, his wellbeing and physique was very upright and appropriate, something that was admirable and commendable. In fact, a request by the mum for junior to visit the health facility or pick and drop something ignited gossip and conversation among the peers and other person on the acts and attitudes father and mother.

Junior's second cycle education begun upon the passing of his common entrance examination at the Catholic Boys Secondary School. The process started with the negotiation for the boarding fee payment, clothing and stipends for his upkeeps. This process caught up with legal teams and opinion leaders from both sides of the parents. In situations like this where parents are high with joy to celebrate the excellence of their wards, father –health colleague then comes in to take control of the son and further proposes in a grand style the cost-sharing module for the ward.

Legal considerations are positioned to provide the son an education that could be peaceful and enjoyable. But to the amusement of the maternal team, that father, the highly esteemed health professional stands on the grounds to provide just the school fee and nothing more. Reason being that he has numerous children at the second cycle to take care off. The lessons are that several males have used their positions, stature and wealth to woo numerous ladies into relationship just to push the burden of upkeep on the women. The principle of 'occasional remittance' towards the son becomes abortive for the payment of fees. In all the several appeals to have the father change the stands and assist or provide some additional support becomes futile. The mother and the maternal lineage at this instance manage to provide all the social needs and academic requirements of their son. So what then happens if the maternal lineage is handicap and can therefore not be in the position to provide for the needs of the child?

Occupational practice as point of call for spouses has been adjudge as the best means of supporting one another in the life journey for partners and persons in relationship. In the Akan culture, total dependency or the reliance on other persons and partners breed bluffs and show-off by the dependable. Perhaps, females who are in gainful employment or have one trade or the other and are able to raise some financial resources are able to honour the challenges of nurturing and raising children. It is most appropriate if female's family and sibling are wealthy and for that matter are able to complement the efforts of spouses. After all the Akan matrimonial inheritance system that offers children the opportunity to be with their mother's lineage also informs their males to support their female siblings and their children at the expense of their own children. This practice though is on a down slide today due education and affectionate, traces still linger on in the indigenous communities and traditional cultural homes.

Junior proceeds to the tertiary cycle to study technical and vocational education specializing in industrial design and production in a prestigious university in Ghana. In Ghana, tertiary education brings prestige and honour to families and several homes. As a diplomat country, paper qualification takes precedence over technical skill and knowledge, therefore being a university graduate was honourable. Since parents, the father and mother are all tertiary products, the pride of having their son proceed to become a tertiary lad was reality and joy to them. Pursuing tertiary education in state university in Ghana requires some financial injections from parents and guardians.

Although the state of Ghana provides infrastructure and salaries for teaching and technical support staff, it becomes incumbent for students to assist with their feeding, clothing, transportation and other learning materials costs. Lifestyle and cross-cultural practices add to the cost of living on tertiary campuses. Technical skills and competencies coupled with traditional African knowledge and lessons on other humanity theorization had been imbibed in the new tertiary lad. These competencies culminated in several academic and competency honours and awards.

Faculty members and students both esteemed the technical accuracies and competencies of Junior to the extent that at the final part of his undergraduate programme he was offered accelerated admission to the faculty's post graduate programme pending his selection as a demonstrator in the department. Junior graduates with double Honours from the prestigious university to the admiration of the maternal lineage and his grandpa throws a banquette for his achievement and performance. As the adage goes 'good flavour permeates the entire environment.

The academic excellence and the good technical works of the Junior traverse to the hearing of the father's nooks and crannies and these offers him the opportunity to bluff to the community the fruits of his exploits forgetting the fact that his contribution towards the acclaimed exploit was negligible and of insignificant demeanor. Yet, the father goes bragging about his germ that has taken of his academic steps. But science has proven that, a child bears the trace of the mother's intelligent quota that is how come several male university dons do not have their children proceed to the tertiary cycle.

**Professional Excellence**
Junior has managed to carve a niche for himself in the area of design and manufacturing. He brings out in his community brilliant and tailor made models that have caught fast on with the hospitality and the media industries. He reorganized the facades halls and lounge of several hotels, corporate edifices and private mansion into world class properties and tourist sites. His professional excellence pulled to his side great connoisseurs of design with technical flair.

Junior after some number of years of professional practice and teaching in a Community Technical University, and with the help of his connoisseurs establishes a competency based product design and manufacturing institute to train the teeming youth of Ghana in production. He then gives back to his community what they have planted in him. The institute was named after the father. There is an Akan adage that says that; 'buy for yourself a dog and name it after your enemy so it can remind you of your predicaments as you call it'. So that root you left behind has become that germ that prides the community, family and individuals.

Good family, good association and good community systems allows the survival and the growth of all persons and their community as well. The physical world is limited by what is shrouded in the future. Men are limited by sight and therefore are unable to perceive accurately, it is only the cosmic world that has some revelations to the future of people. Let us keep our own and nurture them for tomorrow, let us negotiate for the best if we are unable to make it work for us for all humans are the best treasures of the world. Welcome home Junior.

## Symbolism of Root to Story

The flamboyant nature of the acacia root stock heads informs one of the presences of esteems—prestige, physiques, skills, titles, wealth and others that exist in institutions and organizations of work which becomes an enticement for relationship. These esteems that fuels relationships may become means of blessing or curse to the relationship. Therefore issues that may arise of these have the ability to rock the relations and cause the performance or otherwise. Off-springs of such relationships may not attain the full benefits of the parents and may suffer their displeasure and support. The natural umber and burnt umber colour scheme has the penchant to hold dirt and filth and make it deceptive to onlooker and neighbours. This makes it difficult for one to predict the bearers mind and being.

The smooth and firm base of the root structure informs one of the well being and soundness of the presumed esteem and proper relationship in a work place. But over estimated relationship may prescribe the grandest of the esteems and the valuables that exist towards the vulnerable and the less esteemed in the work place. Therefore, occupational romance although may breed efficiency, advocacy, recreation and pleasure, it also has the tendency to rock productivity, persons and family.

The 'Espouse' root educates us on the lesson that, when a person who has endured denial and rejection from his/her intended spouse and lover or parents but comes to terms with the assistance of the cosmic world, she or he will be able move into prominence through the power of the Almighty God.

# CHAPTER THREE
# CAMPAIGNER: HEAD PORTERISM
## 'Appampem somm'

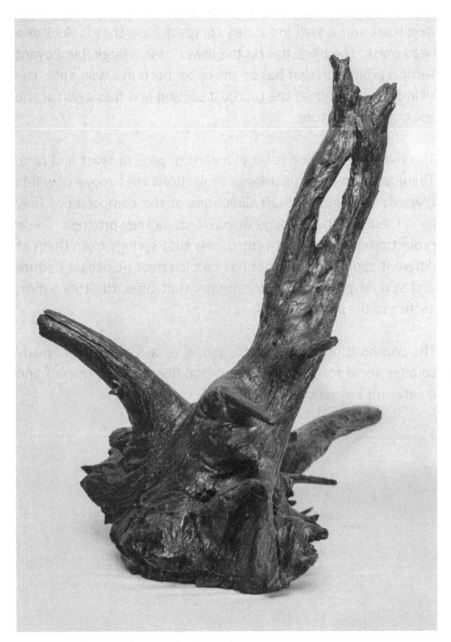

Plate three: Campaigner

'Campaigner' is a found traditional African hard tree root that has been fixed—cleaned, trimmed and varnished for interior and exterior decoration. The traditional root that has umber or reddish-brown colour has several projections that move in diverse directions and a well grounded compact base that looks like a head mask. The piece has on the lower base a large flamboyant vertical projection that has on the upper portion a twin-split. The twin-split separate at the topmost section and fuss again at the apex of the structure.

This middle projection is set in a vertical pose of twist and turn. There are two additional large projections that move upwards towards the right and left directions of the composition. They have their root heads bend downwards as they progress. These projections have smaller protrusions that springs from them at different spot. The hard root has tactile stream-like bark texture and several protruded knot stumps that offer the tree a firm anchor to the soil.

The composition suggests the action of a 'Campaigner' ready to offer some form of entrepreneurial liberation to oneself and create employment to mankind.

Figure Three; Campaigner

55

'Campaigner' Saadea, a Senior High School graduate and a social advocate, had from her infancy the desire to own and operate a multi-lateral enterprise that could offer the teeming youth of her locality that type of employment they have long been waiting for. As an indigene of the upper portion of Ghana, she observed that certain cultural practices, which included introduction of formal western education was targeted at the male children. Domestic chores were limited to only the females, early marriage was prescribed for the infant females and the subjugating of females to harsh labour and excessive humility that affects the ingenuity and potential talent of the womanhood.

Saadea further observed that, religious aggression and suppression that was targeted at the females made them to absorb and imbibe the full Mohammedan doctrine without having the opportunity to question or reason through the lines of life. The economic deprivation and financial meltdown, coupled with commercial dispossession made it extremely complicated to survive in their own terrain. Moreover, in all these, the harsh climatic condition, seasonal farming, persistent famine, lack of role models and others have made it impossible for the teeming youth to stay within their traditional setting and develop their dreams and visions to the betterment of their family and future.

Saadea, a teenager of excellent stature, slender and tall but with moderate curves and contours possesses a fair and untainted skin. Her bulging eyes, round nose and thick lips set in between the smooth running cheeks smoothened her pleasant facial. Like an African sculpture piece that represent fertility, her elongated cranium, balled chin and long-coiled firm neck project the energy and strength that dwells in her. Saadea's elongated torso that showcases the compact and protuberance breast, stretched flat tummy, pronounced genitals and carefully carved bulgy-buttocks that sit on the sturdy-brawny legs which carry her structure expresses her energetic readiness to function actively in the world as a porter, a trade that for some period has been attractive to the Saharan youth. Back in school, Sadaae had the flair in all the commercial subjects and had excelled in other subjects including accounting and management. Procurement and Store Keeping were the subjects that offered and won her most accolades. She was the torch bearer and had received annual awards throughout her study period as a Senior High School student.

Saadea's excellent reading skills, diction and the ability to pronounce difficult words accurately made her to be admired greatly by her teachers and peers in the senior high she attended. Her excellent performance in spelling at the basic school gave her the opportunity to visit the capital city- Accra for a 'Spelling Bee' competition. In the capital city, Saadea was astonished at the colourful, huge concrete and steel jungle that had been carefully planted on the ground as domestic and commercial accommodations. Additionally, Saadea was astonished at the fast and sleek moving vehicles as well as the huge passenger buses and haulage trucks that were used to move humans and goods from one destination to another.

She witnessed young and middle aged ladies and gentlemen who were smartly dressed and moving swiftly as possible to their intended locations. In fact, she observed several and different types of ladies head coiffure and facial and skin paintings or make-ups that made people look super human and attractive to stare at. These and other sites and scenes made Saadea wished to live in Accra and possibly work there as an entrepreneur. As a finalist in the spelling competition, she gained enough confidence and hoped to study in the business university in Accra.

On her journey back home, and as she sat in the posh tourist bus provided by the 'Spelling Bee' Organizers to take teams from Koforidua through Kumasi to the up north, they drove past Medina Market in Accra and Aboabo and the central market in the Ashanti region and to her amusement there were several Saharan girls and boys plying one trade or the other to improve themselves and their family's social status. She got worried about these menaces and could not comprehend the benefits at hand since to her education held the keys to success.

Back home, after the spelling competition, Saadea had kept the communication flow with the friends she made while an Accra through the post. She had gotten several photographs from them on where they live, how they live, where they visit and what they do while at home. Information including sites and scenes of home and abroad made her wonder why her family and community lived in such situation while people down south lived in wonderful houses, walked on polished floors and sat in nice cars and not in sorry situation such as raffia and mud huts, dusty and dry streets, and ride on rickety motor bikes and donkeys.

To her, their world was a fifth world since she had read that even Accra the capital city of Ghana is classified a third class city by the world standard. These and others attractions including the walking and talking styles of the ladies and the freedom ascribed to ladies, the posh houses women lived in and sleek cars they drove, had inspired her to make it her ambition to live and work in Accra or any of the big cities someday soon.

Despite the stern cultural practices addressed at women, preference of higher education for only the males, the daunting domestic chores for the females, adherence of early marriage towards females, strict religious suppression targeting females, high economic deprivation, unforgivable commercial dispossession, uncompromising harsh climatic condition, persistent famine, lack of sufficient academic female role models and others, Saadea was able to obtain distinction in all her commercial and language subjects, and good passes in science and mathematics.

This performance could offer Saadea admission to any of the prestigious tertiary institutions in Ghana as a business student. Inspite of Saadea's outstanding performance at the West Africa Senior Secondary School Examination (WASSCE), the cultural practice of not allowing females to proceed on the ladder of education, coupled with the financial quagmire of the family, Saadea had to abandon her dreams temporarily and pursue other trades that were outside her ambitions.

These and other pressures propelled Saadea to announce to her parents for the first time her intent to pursue greener pasture in the capital city just as her female peers had done earlier. This decision of Saadea and the inherent cultural beliefs of her family in a clear manifestation of that anger, the father sacked or threw her out of his home as an outcast. This action of the father made her venerable to the influence of others who had same ambitions. Just as what Saadea was going through, her mother had no option but to tow the line of the father else she may have to follow Saadea into the wilderness.

Saadea's plea and that of the extended families and neighbours for mercy from the father did not yield any fruits. For weeks, she was on her own and could sneak home for support from the mother only at the blind side of the father. Saadea had no option but to accompany the others with same predicament and the city been to to Kumasi.

Her journey to the capital city—Accra— in search of greener pastures required some parental blessings and as well as financial injections or support just to make her progress effectively in relation to her passion for higher education, professionalism and financial growth for the betterment of the family's financial fortunes forever. But, how can the parents genuinely release their precious daughter into the wonderland? A place they perceive to contain lot of social blights, cultural influences, religious freedom and sovereignty, cash flights and ostentatious life style and high immoral tendencies that put women and girls at high risks.

Saadea's plight, just like the excellent performance of another Saharan girl child who had A's in all her West Africa Senior Secondary School Examination (WASSCE) at the previous examination but could not attract any scholarship to proceed on the ladder of education, journeying down south for help had become the order of the day. Political leadership from the Saharan region had not done enough to curb this menace. They are not rolling enough scholarship schemes to attract and retain the girls in the tertiary institutions. Although, secondary education is virtually free for all the Saharan youth, getting the girls in secondary schools was a bit challenging let alone the tertiary.

The young and active working forces were also putting aside their quest to seek higher education in pursuit of mirages of wealth through the menial jobs from the middle and southern regions an act that was hardly attainable. Saadea manages to meet a city been to, a Saharaian who works in the south and has come home to showcase her fortunes to the admiration of her community. She then strikes a deal to assist in making her passion to stay and work in the south come through. The date for the journey is arranged and preparations were also put in place. Saadea sneaks with the city been to, the Kumasi Burger and the travel agent to Kumasi to undertake some menial jobs as startup. She stays and works in a local restaurant known in the Ghanaian parlance as 'chop bar'. She worked as a hand responsible for the clearing of tables and washing of plates and pans.

Kumasi, the second capital of Ghana has an overwhelming buoyant and brisk commercial tendency that allows for some vociferous expression. The vigorous and rigorous life-style in Kumasi was another thing to contend with. Her almost a quarter of a year experience in the city exposed her to the rancor, hustle and bustle of the middle belt. But her upbringing, calm nature and academic persona made her to suffocate in Kumasi. Upon this, she made several phone calls to her 'Spelling Bee' colleagues to link her up to Accra where she desired most and felt her ambitions could best be achieved. Finally, she relocates to Accra to ply a trade as a head potter popularly known as Kayayo.

Saadea, finally wins the attention of one of the 'Spelling Bee' girls 'Adolley' who then appeal to the parents to offer Saadea some Ghanaian Cedis (money) to enable her move from Kumasi to Accra and also secure for her a space in their boys' quarters or domestic help room. Adolley, the only girl child of the parents is born to a middle-class family that lives in an enclosed estate gated community. Her parents drive a fairly home-used saloon car and have a house help that undertakes housekeeping chores for the family. Saadea was made to put up with the house help in the boys quarters as the facility had a two-tier bed for two.

Saadea's upbringing, calm nature and academic persona made her win the attention of the new family at least for the period that she lived with them. She was served with two meals a day and a stipend to buy some personal needs. She was entrusted with some few errands to keep her active until she found a job. Her errands took her to the Agbobloshie and Mallam Atta markets where she met with lots of the Saharan girls and boys who have come down to seek for greener pastures. She later joins the trade of head potter as the immediate option. She then had to commutes from her gated community to the market place where she plies her trade everyday and back.

Saadea's activities as a head potter in the market place brought her closer to several middle-class people who had come to purchase one or two items for their homes and food joints. Her stature and affable nature coupled with truthfulness made her to win lots of such middle-class elites to her blossom. She had the opportunity to perform her trade to their admiration. As middle-class elites and career-women or business ladies of the mid-ages, their set up targets could not be interlaced with some of these errands to accomplish their desired domestic goals, hence their dependence on some reliable Kayayos.

Saadea in some instances had the opportunity to take requests from her clients and deliver to their homes and offices for a fee, these requests for purchases and deliveries grew the clientele base of Saadea as several customers made recommendation to their friends about her services and reliability. She occasionally joined some clients on Sundays to perform laundry and cleaning services when she had no errand to run. These and other services she rendered gained her a sizeable client base of which she alone could no longer undertake.

After a year of practice, Saadea had recruited and trained five girls and two boys into her brand 'Saadea Services'. These girls and boys could perform same errands at the beacon of Saadea for a fee. 'Brand Saadea' had permeated the circles of the elite class and their confidence on her services made their visits to the market places an issue of the past since their reliability was gaining roots. Saadea attracted one of her client, a graphic artist' who professionally elevated Brand Saadea with some corporate branding such as well-designed Lacoste T' shirts, skirts and scarfs for females, caps and trousers for the males and sneakers for all. This conspicuous green, yellow and white colour scheme with the inscription 'Saadea Serves You Better—Saadea Cares' did the magic. Additionally, her designer provided her with business call cards and receipt slips and packaging bags that bore the famous inscription Saadea Serves You Better — Saadea Cares.

Saadea services got her into the famous University of Ghana, Legon campus for the first time in her life. A phone call from a female Professor in the Business School requested for a 'Shop and Deliver' service. The request was for Saadea to deliver in person since the Professor had heard of the entrepreneurial niche she had carved for herself. Saadea arrived on the university campus and took the direction to the Business School and the Professor's office. Saadea's admiration grew stronger since for the first time she had encountered a high profile female role model. In her mind, the Business School was her most inspired final point for academic ladder, and that her pursuit was to make it a reality. Saadea met with the Professor introduced herself and delivered the request to the client—the female University Professor.

The items were thoroughly inspected to establish the veracity of the transaction before the payment was effected. These and other inspections confirmed the much heard of the Saadea Brand. Saadea issued the payment slip and added her business card. This influenced and affected the light-heart of the University Professor to delve into her, the academic and social background of Saadea. To her astonishment, Saadea an SHS graduate rose from the Saharan region of the country and had come to Accra to do menial work to fund her education in the university. Saadea was most qualified to be on the management programme of the Business School. The Professor had a case study to share with her students. In fact, Saadea won her admiration and she promised to ensure the enrollment of Sadea on the Marketing Programme of the Business School when she was ready to and applied for admission to continue her schooling or education.

Brand Saadea had grown beyond expectations. For two years, Saadea had shown a demonstrable skill in wealth creation and the can do spirit. This skill confirmed the 'Yes I Can' slogan that Obama the former president of the United States of America had offered the black community of America to rise from their slumber, propose something and believe in it, and make it fruitful to mankind. In all these successes Saadea still put up with her foster home. This allowed Adolley's parents to permitted Saadea to raise a mini container along the façade of their house as an office accommodation for the Saadea Services.

Saadea Services had become an inspiration to Adolley so much that during her academic recess from the university, she assisted Saadea in the management of her venture. In the third year, Saadea gained admission into University of Ghana Business, a dream she had longed for and was a student and a client of a Professor. A dream she had longed for. A dream come through, something that had moved her from the north to the south. While in school, Saadea had appointed an assistant to assist in the running of the brand.

Though in school, Saadea kept an eye on the brand, took calls and directed partners to the calls to shop and deliver accordingly. Academic lessons and modules had sharpened Saadea and her business. She understood and applied some of the case studies to the advantage of her venture. While in school, she had used her affable nature to extend her business to the university community and the affluent students. In all these, Saadea made some additional income to pay her university fees, partners and remit her parents and make some savings to expand the business. Saadea graduates from the Business School with Second Class Upper Division and return full time to Saadea Services as the CEO and to apply the acquired and enhanced skills and knowledge to the benefit of the business and the clients.

CEO Saadea, brings onboard the Saadea Services Limited the entire skill and knowledge she has acquired from her University's Business School. She has taken the business to the next level by off loading part of her shares to raise additional financial injection. She offers Adolley a minute share and makes one of the parents a board member. Saadea advises the share holders to expand the company by adding two offices one in East Legon, a prestigious community in Accra where the wealthy resides and the other in Abobloshie Market. She then advises the relocation of the office on the Adolley's premises to Kaneshie Market which is at the western part of Accra.

All offices were to recruit two workers each to take care of administration and marketing. In addition, she proposed a road map to recruit errand boys and girls from ages fifteen to twenty in the first a year of her institutional expansion regime. This was to take care of their services delivery. Within the first three years of operation, Brand Saadea had over sixty errands boys and girls serving a client base of seven hundred. She had procured twenty motor bicycles and ten tricycles for distribution and carting of waste from client homes and offices.

Within the first five years, Brand Saadea had become a major distributor of grocery and representative of two giant shopping malls responsible for the dispatch of groceries and some electrical gargets. Additionally, she had become a major player in the procurement sector procuring and distributing fresh vegetables, live and dressed poultry products, cereals and legume and all types of bread that was produced from her bakery. Brand Saadea had grown a client base of more than one thousand and since she could not meet all the client's needs she moved into mobile vendor of her products using the services of food carts and food trucks.

Good family system, good association and good entrepreneurial systems allow for the survival and growth of all persons and the community as well. The physical world is always limited by what is covered for the future. Dr Mensa Otabil an astute preacher, the Head Pastor of the International Central Gospel Church (ICGC) in his presentation to his listeners once said; 'the Almighty God has made all things for man and has covered them. But it will only take His grace to get man discovered or uncovered them for the benefit of mankind. Humans are limited by sight and therefore are unable to perceive accurately, it is only the cosmic world that has some revelations to the future of people.

Let us keep our vision and nurture them for tomorrow, let us dream big but start small and keep the pace of performance. Negotiate for the best if you can, make it work if you must, for if it must be done then it must be done well, a popular theme or slogan for an Insurance Entity of the Methodist Church of Ghana. All humans are the best treasures of the world. Welcome to the Saharan region Saadea! You are the model to treasure!

## Symbolism of Root to Story
The mask-like piece presents a rising movement from like structures that offer support to each other in an attempt to seek some entrepreneurial advocacy and liberation among the marginalized. The compact base of the composition and the projections rising from it suggest the attempt to render support to each other in spite of the capabilities and competencies that exits among equals. The rising but bowed projections at the left and right of the composition suggest the natural and cultural obstacles that emanate from the geographical area.

The continual dryness of the savanna and the harsh climatic regime make it seemingly impossible for the inhabitants to break through economically and commercially to their advantage.

Hence the social down turn of the indigenes that calls for their migration to the south. The mid-split at the topmost part of the middle projection and their further fusion at the apex depict the possibility for one to succeed even if there are artificial and natural obstacles that are bound to occur as one attempt make strides. A break from ones shell and a possible leap into the fertile and commercially buoyant regions are likely to allow for some manifestations of one's ambition and vision. If you focus on your ambition there is always the possibility to break through in life's journey.

The 'Campaigner' root educates the youth on lessons which emphasis that persons who have undergone denial, suppression and rejection from their parents, community and generation but are able to resist these odds will come to prominence with the assistance of the cosmic world and the Almighty God.

# CHAPTER FOUR
## PUGILIST: HEAD JANITORISM
### 'Ahomsantsinye'

Plate Four: Pugilist

'Pugilist' is a found Acacia root that has been fixed— cleaned, trimmed and varnished for interior and exterior decoration. The wood has burnt umber and ocher colours that are obtained from the natural scheme of the root. The Acacia root is composed in a swift motion pose. The piece provides a compact lower portion that sits on a tripod base. The tripod represents the legs that are set in the form of leap to action. It is composed of a leaping front leg, an intermediate step leg and an out-stretched back leg suggesting a previously landed step.

The upper most portion of the root structure has three vertical projections that connect to a back-tilted trunk which serves as the torso to the figure. These vertical projections represent the two raised hands and head that depict an upward posture of a figure sets to seek clean the filth from a height. It suggests the action of a Pugilist ready to step into some form of occupational and social liberation to human race inspite of formal western higher education.

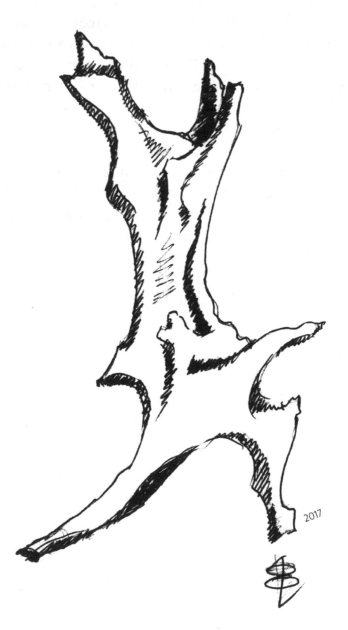

Figure Four: Pugilist

Pugilist Kojo, a Junior High School graduate and the elder son of the parents had a poor social support system from his infancy. His desire to be a prominent person in future was the indispensable inspiration from his earlier days. Although the parents had separated while he was very young, the father, a migrant worker in the mines, was a chauffeur who owned and operated a taxi cab during the weekends. He occasionally had some few counsels for him to stay focus and pursue his wish for prominence only through a genuine path.

He always asked him not to depart from God's words, be respectful, truthful and serviceable to all persons especially the elderly. He also asked him to be hardworking and modest in living, since modesty was the hallmark for excellence. The mother a known petty trader and very offensive, and had the pungent of quarreling and fighting at the slightest provocation. She was witty, greedy, self centered and wanted anything that belonged to others. This made her to indulge her other children into pilfering and shoplifting, a behaviour that always got them into the grips of the law.

Kojo's father sought permission from the court to possess and live with him from the age of nine. This was to curtail the influence of the mother's behaviour on him and allow for a proper upbringing. He had remarried and settled as a responsible family man. The new wife, a basic school teacher and a daughter of a priest was very affable but a great disciplinarian. She loved Kojo and took him as her son. Kojo also embraced her and took her words of advice and instructions in good faith. This propelled him to be loved by all in their community including the friends and bosses of the father.

At fifteen, kojo had graduated from the Junior High School but could not make the appropriate mark needed to enter into any

Senior High School. Entry into Senior High School in the south was extremely competitive. Very few vacancies were available to the populous youth, based on this, it was easy to find several adolescents idling about for want of Senior High School education, trade and skills, a requisite for gainful employment. Technical and vocational education and training had not caught up with the elites, the policy formulators and implementers were also a mockery in the community since it was perceived that only the low intelligent quotient persons were fit or qualified for that type of education and training.

There were few multi-lateral enterprises that could offer the teeming youth of the community that type of employment they have longed for. As an indigene of the southern sector, Kojo observed that certain cultural practices, which included introduction of formal western education and academism was targeted at only the children who had shown early academic potentiality while apprenticeship, farming and domestic chores were reserved for the partial and low academics. Moreover the subjugating of infants and children to harsh labour and excessive exploitation affect the ingenuity and potential talents of the youth.

Kojo further observed that, early marriage and teenage pregnancy which was high among the youth oblique the opportunities and chances of success of his contemporary. And since the devil finds work for the idle hands Kojo opted to accompany the father to the work place to enable him learn his trade and also create some acquaintance among the work force.

Kojo's father, a senior heavy duty dumper driver, had enormous exposure and experience in risk and steep hill maneuvering. He was preferred by the mining authorities for his skill in heavy duty mechanical technician. As a cherished worker with good character and humility, he commanded some reasonable respect among the work force and management. The introduction of Kojo into the workplace as an apprentice in the auto cleaning and service center was warmly embraced by all and sundry. The headman, a South African white liked and loved Kojo for his calmness and semblance of the father. Kojo was enlisted as an apprentice and his work commenced the next day.

He was provided a set of safety apparels and shown his cabinet. As a teachable person, he exhibited a high sense of duty and dedication to his training and assigned responsibility. Six months into his apprenticeship training, he was able to demonstrate a higher level of skills and competencies in auto body interior and exterior washing and cleaning. He also received some skills training in carpets and furniture cleaning and maintenance. As a calm and soft spoken person, he attached much care and diligence his work and sought to provide all the necessary attention required of his delivery.

A year into his training, he again received training in laundry and fabric care, and placed in charge of the newly acquired industrial washing machine assigned to wash the clothes or apparels of worker. In the second year of his training, Kojo was nominated to visit South Africa to attend further training in the handling of some new laundry and fabric care, and care and maintenance of laundry equipment procured for the mines.

The one month intensive training provided him with a Corporate Certificate in Laundry and Fabric Care and an Ordinary Certificate in Laundry and Fabric Equipment Maintenance. In addition, he was offered a gold certificate to represent the manufacturers in Ghana as the sales and installation consultant for a client who purchased from the company.

He could buy at ten percent discount and visit the company's premises once annually for International Standard Order (ISO) license renewal and laundry technician upgrading. Kojo's return from overseas to the mines brought some elevation to his status. He also introduced some changes to his unit. His headman placed him in charge of the laundry of the expatriate and higher senior management and their families. This was due to his higher skill and competency in special fabric and high quality clothes. Kojo's excellence at services delivery in the mines as apprentice could not earn him a permanent employme nt. The opportunity offered him to travel overseas to acquire technical proficiencies and certifications could also not secure him the needed permanent opportunity. Moreover his father's cloud as a respected senior driver could also not secure him permanent staff opportunity in the Mining Company.

Five years into the service with the Mines, the CEO of the Mining Company mines approaches Kojo to discuss exit plans from the mines and informs him of decision to establish a multi-lateral all-purpose Laundry and Janitorial Service Center, and expresses his intention to partner with him to run the establishment. The CEO had earlier engaged Kojo's father on the partnership and business deal for the son. Kojo's father had shown concerns and referred the deal to the son since he is a young adult. Kojo conferred with the father and the Unit Head on the deal from the CEO, but both of them stated as a matter of fact that, since he was not a permanent staff, but had served the mines duly as per the agreement of his overseas training, he could exit the mines for another offer. However, since the Mining Company had no plans of recruiting washer-men and janitors any more, they all advised that the offer from the CEO could equally be a good deal for his sustenance and future based.

After a considerable period of time and as the deal time was about to elapse, Kojo approached the Recruitment Officer of the Mining Company to inform him of his intention to join another establishment since the mines has no plans for his janitorial and washerman carrier. The officer engaged him thoroughly to ascertain the benefits thereof. Upon a lengthy discussion he pulled out some partnership agreement documents to guide his negotiation, blessed him and offered him the necessary assistance and direction to claim his severance award as per the condition of service for casual workers and trainees. His announcement to disengage and join another establishment came as a surprise to the workers since it was perceived that he had had a better opportunity with the mines to the extent that even as a trainee, the management of the mines extended several courtesies to him as the preferred janitor and washerman of the management and senior members.

A grand opening ceremony is organized to usher into the community the biggest and modern janitorial and laundry service in the community. This grand ceremony was graced by the numerous CEOs of the community, elites, chiefs, middle class managers, business owners and operators of small and middle scale miners and the entire community. On that occasion Kojo was introduced as a managing partner and the supervisor of this world class establishment. He and his work force demonstrated to the audience the effectiveness and the efficiency of their facility and skills. The facility had a service center where they serviced and replaced parts of domestic washing machines. It also had an automotive service center that took care of radiators, greasing and lubrication.

The facility also had a relaxing bar and a snack shop that entertained clients and the community. Since Kojo has had several engagements with the South African company that sold and assembled the equipment for the establishment, he understands and operates them efficiently. The first six months of operation, saw the facility attracting several clientele from near and far. The attracted clients were from the mining sector that brought their vehicles and clothes for washing and servicing. Severally, they were able to establish deals with transport companies to wash and service their vehicles. Numerous private and family car owners had won their admirations to wash and service their cars and cloths.

Two years into their operations, the partnership had attracted a huge clientele that they required additional space and equipment to expand their facility and service. They therefore procured two vehicle mounted washing equipments for outdoor services especially the washing of surface mining equipment such as excavators and crushers that could not move into their facility for servicing. They also procured an automobile lubricating servicing vehicle for outdoor and site services. Two additional stationed car washing machines were mounted to improve upon their services and waiting on time for clients. Three years into their operations and services, they were able to pay their debts, procured a water tanker to improve their outdoor washing services and also to supply portable water to the communities at a reduced fee. The partnership was impressed upon to venture into septic emptier services. Two septic emptiest were added onto their service line.

Within the three years of operation, the partnership had offered over fifty employment opportunities to the indigenes and settlers of the communities. Ten out this work force were former mining staffs who were on retirement. These included administrative staff who had previously worked under the CEO. These people had greater understanding of the CEO's vision and direction. This team included the Employment Officer who counseled Kojo to go along with the CEO for the venture.

Four years into the operations of the partnership, Kojo was able to convince his partners in South Africa to open a franchise in their community so as to sell and service domestic and industrial washing machines and their accessories and consumables. This initiative got the South Africa partners to visit the community to undertake some feasibility studies for the venture. The positive nature of the study made it possible the company to establish two shops in the country, one in the community and the other in the capital city. The CEO and Kojo were giving the management of the community shop but the capital city shop was directly under the supervision of the South African Company.

Both shops performed very well and saw some expansion and face lift. Both shops performed very well due to the fact that they moved into sales and services of electronic gadgets such as televisions, digital receivers, fridges, sound systems, cookers, kitchen and domestic equipment. The two shops were expanded and given face-lift befitting their brand. Kojo sought employment for two of his basic school mates who had graduated from the university with honours in Accounting with Computing and Marketing with Strategic Management to join their management team. Although these former basic school peers have climbed the ladder of education far and above of Kojo, at the time they entered the job market, the business skill, favour and honour of Kojo was over and above their imagination. A preacher had once said that the favour of God is always beyond human expectation. These and other university graduates employed by Kojo and the CEO had to put their skills and expertise to the advantage of the establishment in exchange of remunerations.

Ten years into the operations of the partnership, the CEO, Kojo's partner, took the final leave to South Africa to undertake family leadership. As the elder son of the parents, leadership had come to him due to absence of the father. He therefore equalized the shares to fifty percent  ownership and offered Kojo the leadership role while he sat afar to observe the operations through a rigorous internal and external audit system that had been put in place. While in the home country, the CEO established a similar venture to occupy him. He invited Kojo to assist in establishing the venture during his annual leave period. While in South Africa, he offered an opportunity for Kojo to undergo a leadership and management training workshop to sharpen his skills. He acquired practical skills in financial management and human relations, business growth and sustenance, personal management and self glooming.

All these were factors that to the CEO affected the growth and sustenance of businesses in Ghana and Africa. Kojo returned home equipped to steer the affairs of the partnership and to the expectation of his partner. Two years into his leadership role, Kojo managed to maintain their market share despite new competitors. He managed to establish a mini branch in his home town as an attempt to create some employment for the youth there. He extended further to the next regional capital with some of their ageing equipment and ordered for modern ones for the parent company's operations. Four years into his leadership role saw the CEO offloading his total shares to Kojo. This was to enable the CEO concentrate on the South African venture and make some space for Kojo to take up the responsibilities. Kojo then took over the entity and became the new CEO, a role he never dreamt of from his infancy. Although Kojo had become the new CEO he never severed the relationship between himself and his former boss (CEO) and partner, because the CEO saw the potential in him and brought him up to the success he had attained without a Ghanaian pesewa from his own.

Human beings are always limited by vision and the occurrences of the moment. We, therefore, are unable to distinguish precisely talent and wisdom from academic excellence. People may not show great academic strength from their start but may excel in other facets of life. It is only the cosmic world that has some disclosure to the future of people. Let us keep our vision and nurture them for tomorrow. Negotiate for the best if you can, make it work if you must, for if it must be done then it must be done well. All persons have the best treasures in them and they must be well natured and unearth for the benefit of the world. Welcome to the Fante land Kojo. You are the model to peruse.

# CHAPTER FIVE
# CRUSADER: CHIEF DIVERISM
## Insumudɔhen

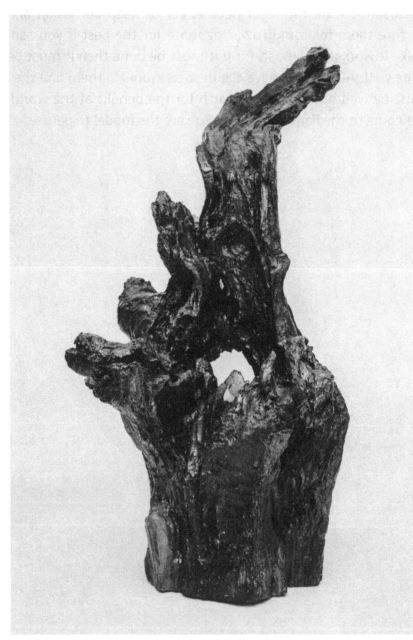

Plate Five: Crusader

'Crusader' is a found root of an indigenous tree that has been fixed—cleaned, trimmed and varnished for interior and exterior decoration. The wood has burnt umber and ocher colours that are obtained from the natural scheme of the root. The piece has combination of vertical projections and perforation that renders Acacia root in a pottered cauliflower pose and portrays it into a gracious posture. It provides a compact cylindrical lower portion on which sits blossom roots heads. The piece projects a group of aquatic creatures springing from a pivoting base towards diverse directions to pursue their prey.

The upper most portion of the root structure has several vertical projections that connect to the base which serves as the receptacle to the creatures. These vertical projections represent the effort to survive after undertaking a diving activity from the basin of the water body. It suggests the action of a 'Crusader' ready to step into some form of occupational and social liberation into the human race despite the lack of proper parental guidance and formal western education.

Figure Five: Crusader

Crusader Kwamivi, a Basic School dropout and the only son of the mother, had an enhanced lard and prop-up system from his birth. He was destined for outstanding future as the father had planned and wished for him. He was the requisite for success and inspiration for his parents from the initial days. Nevertheless, a wedge into the relationship of the parents created a hitch that got his destiny thrown unto the downwards. Although the parents had estranged relationship while he was juvenile, the father, a professional teacher at the basic level also owned and operated a confectionery and provision store on one of the high streets of their community. The store supported his activity and helped raise his family.

Although the father, a known teacher was very academic, eloquent and knowledgeable but his alcoholic tendency prevented him from keeping a watchful eye on his only child. This made his responsibility as a father an issue of neglect and scam. His alcoholic tendency made him unattractive to the opposite sex, lose his self esteem and respect in the community. As a person suffering from alcoholism, he could do very little to nurture the son, as such he created a wayward behaviour for Kwamivi.

The mother, an ostentatious and glitzy person was very religious and hard working. She was predisposed to witty and scam persons, and easily falls to swindlers and persons of humorous behaviour. Although her religious upbringing had an impact on her psycho-socio life style, her fickle minded predisposition made her extremely vulnerable. As an unmarried young lady with one child but not in her possession, she went about her commercial duties as brisk as possible to the amusement of the community. She could turn around all misfortune and situations into greater business opportunity and made lot of gains. Although she had a child, she was not directly responsible for his upkeep and raising, she therefore had all the opportunities to pursue her amorous relationship. This also offered her the chance to go about her trading activities without any sense of child responsibilities in and out of her home.

As beautiful as she was, her Ghanaian and African features were non-resistible, highly receptive and able to pull any person including women to her attention and attraction. The showcasing of her elaborate neck and arm jewelry fashioned from glass beads and gold and her dangling ear rings put her into a category of her own. Her over exposed bust, bulgy eyes and protruded ball-like buddies or buttocks were the must watched and graceful to the eyes of mankind. Her gracious and elegant calculated steps placed her into the realm of a fashion model. But in all these, she could not connect with the activities of the son and left him to the mercy of the alcoholic father, and the community to nurture.

At age eight, Kwamivi had to witnessed the gruesome death of his father when he was knocked down by a speeding vehicle that did not even stop attend to him. The father was returning from his usual drinking spree when the accident and untimely death occurred. The demised of the father then exposed Kwamivi to the vagaries and vices of the community since the external members of the father's family had gave up on him. Within a couple of months after the death, the father's investments and properties had been looted and shared among the family and friends leaving nothing for him to depend upon. These and other challenges propelled Kwamivi to make a search for the whereabout of his blissful mother.

Adjo, the self-styled fashion model and the mother to Kwamivi had settled down casually with another fashion crazed middle-aged man who plies his trade as a merchant. Although the community in which they were domiciled was located on the banks of a lake, both Adjo and the lover were not fisher folks. It was rather the lover who was involved in the purchase and supply of lobsters and shrimps to hospitality establishments situated or located in the cities. He also supplied fishing gears and accessories to the fisher folks. As if this trade could not suffice him, he was also deeply into the kidnapping and sale of infants and children to operators of fisheries and shrines that were also located on the banks of lake and fishing towns. Kwamivi's reunion with the mother was nothing pleasurable since from infancy he had not jelled or had a good rapport with her.

The community had no educational facility therefore all the kids and youth were uneducated. This did not go well with Kwamivi since his desire was to become a teacher like the father and continue his good works. But as the saying goes "if you go to Rome, you do as the Romans do", Kwamivi had to join the youth of the community to undergo fishing. Through his association with the youth, he acquired the skill of swimming and diving. He also became a master in the dressing and seasoning of fishes and other sea foods as part of the trade. Although the mother tried all means to become that mother that Kwamivi had dreamt of, his new role as a fisher folk had offered him some financial freedom and making him not to depend on the mother, as such, he became wayward and freed to do whatever he deemed fit and appropriate.

There is the adage that says:"spare the rod and spoil the child" this adage does not always become reflective because, change is one thing that is very difficult to adopt in Kwamivi's case or situation. In making a decision to change for the better, one requires an effort that is very purposeful, progressive and directional.

A social coach once said to his mentees "If one does not change he remains in chains, and that a choice you make lives to affect your fortunes. Whatever choice you make, makes your choice a change"

Since Kwamivi had previously been in that kind of uncontrolled and non-nurtured life-style, it was extremely difficult for him to change or change him for the better to meet the wishes of the mother and the mother's lover and step-father. This predicament occasionally got Kwamivi into trouble and rancour with his peers, mother, step-father and others.

At age ten, Kwamivi had become very unmanageable and a truant. He has become sordidly to the extent that the mother's lover (step father) could not contain him and therefore decided to sell him off to a tour operator in a far place just to let him have his peace and space for his amorous relationship with the mother. Hitherto, Kwamivi had demonstrated a deep hatred for the mother's lover and step-father just because he presumed that his presences in the mother's life might have contributed to the neglect and the drinking culture of his late father, something that led to his untimely death.

In an attempt by step-father (or the mother's lover) to perpetuate his intentions, he drew very close to Kwamivi and also upheld his deeds. He created a father-like situation between himself and Kwamivi, and offered him the opportunity to undertake the acts himself and the mother had previously condemned him of. This fostered some trust and affection between them as well as the mother and as a child, he perceived the new relationship as an embracement for better.

There is an adage that goes that; "you cannot see the construct of the mind from the face" and that even when people are smiling with you, there might be some form of bitterness and ill thoughts behind their beautiful eyes. Little did Kwamivi know that this father-like embrace was a cast of a steel net meant mask him ceaselessly. This embraced was an evil ploy and machination meant to trap him so as to sell him off to the tour operator. Put simply, the step-father or mother's lover's only desire for him was evil-intent destruction, not anything good, but unknown to the step-father, the Almighty God had better and not bitter plans for kwamivi.

A day was set for Kwamivi to accompany the mother's lover on a business trip into the inlands water space. The trip was to meet a business tycoon who was affable and affectionate to the plight of school dropouts and engages them for skills training. This gracious arrangement was prearranged outside the domain of the mother—Adjo. Adjo had developed much interest and love for the son and took him for what he was. She had shared much of her aspirations with him just as the father had done earlier. This new love for the son had also come as a result of the paradigm shift that had occurred between the mother's lover and the son. The trust that had brewed between the son and the mother's lover had extended to the mother for the better.

All the three members of the family had embraced themselves with care and love due to the new found rapport with one another. This seemingly positive attitude and overtures had made it possible for them to swim in a pool of ecstasy and sense of belonging. Kwamivi's contribution to the upkeeping of the family was so enormous in relation to his humour, services and goods and rendered financial contributions were much felt. Yet in all these, cynicisms and skepticisms could not be envisioned particularly the evil intended mother's lover. His mother's lover kept his intent to have Kwamivi dispossessed off without the mother's (Adjo) knowledge to him.

The mother's lover could envisage that Kwamivi was in to thwart his chance of swindling Adjo of her wealth and resources, these and other factors accounted for his deep seated dislike and hatred fueling his intention or purpose to sell him off or dislodge him from their midst. The mother's lover agreed with Kwamivi to meet in the next town to proceed on their journey to meet the business tycoon where, he knew will be the beginning and the end of Kwamivi life.

The journey to the business tycoon started with some good pleasantries and felicitation, three other boys joined the journey. The unending journey got them to that part of the country that require the crossing of the overseas lake and dry vast lands that shows indications of water basin. The huge booming sounds of the boats and jet skies were scary and terrifying. For over fifteen minutes the boat they were travelling on had not reached their destination. For a moment they were totally surrounded by the water and that no concrete structure could be identified. These frightening and chilling moments put the courage and bravery of Kwamivi to test. He was almost immersed in fear and contemplated an end to his world. He imagined that life had come to an abrupt end, but in a split of a moment their boat pointed towards the beautiful facility of the business tycoon and as they disembarked, they were welcomed into the facility heavily guarded by the armed men.

Kwamivi and the other boys were welcomed and ushered to their apartments. After three days of interaction and familiarization, the mother's lover could not be seen by his boys, he had completed his deal with the business tycoon and declared them vanquished. The boys had become the property of the tycoon and perpetually sold into slavery and servitude. Their life from that day was a situation of camping, service and exploitation. In the camp were several boys and few girls who were brought from villages and towns that were near and far. They were bathed and offered new identities and names. In the camp were older and younger folks. The camp had several trade and skill centers that were associated with production and sales. Notable of these were the bakery center that provided bread and cake for breakfast in the hospitality industry, the carving craft shop that produced furniture and masks for export, the sewing center that did the crafting of uniforms and apparels for prison inmates, institutions and celebrities.

In addition, was the aquatic and fishing accessories unit specializing in the harnessing of exotic fishes, sea foods, the mining of precious pebbles and river bed silt for construction and also export to oversea countries. This unit trained young boys to be specialists in diving, submerging and submarine activities due to the fact that their tasks were basically to release trapped fishing nets, hooks, lines and the anchors of boats and canoes entangled under the sea bed. In addition to the fishing of exotic fishes and sea foods, they also performed the selection and lifting unpacked and packed fish crates for storage, sales and transportation. As the new boys were taken through the various centers and units of the facility, the operators identified Kwamivi as a very skillful and passionate person in relation to aquatic life because of the way he excelled in diving, submerging, selection of fishes and waning of silt. Though Kwamivi had no formal academic training marine services, his association with his peers at the mother's community offered him the opportunity to maneuvers in water bodies and adapt well to aquatic life, based on these attributes and skills, he was enlisted in this unit.

Though meant for evil, Kwamivi postured himself so well that after two years of stay in the facility, the operator had entrusted him with the responsibility of rescuing colleagues and damaged fishing gears from disaster prone areas under the seabed. He performed his duties so well that for over half a decade no incident was recorded in the facility. His surveillance and high security alertness gained him lots of accolade such as 'Able Seaman', 'No Water' and 'Water Ninja'. He grew into the natural security gang of the facility and was put in naval surveillance and defense squad. As an unmarried youth, he could risk his life for the sustenance of the facility. The marine squad was on regular periods offered military training and schematics to make them physically strong and loyal to the defense and operation of the facility. At age eighteen, Kwamivi had the physique, brand loyalty and attachment to his duties to the extent that he totally forgot his mother and peers back home.

Though Kwamivi had developed some attachment for the mother before joining the facility, the initial slavery and ideological injection infused in him by the facility operators expelled the linkage with his root. He had totally forgotten about himself as an indigene of the parents' lineage. A raid and siege on the facility by an opposing partner raised fear and panic on the operators. The invasion exposed some cracks in their security and generated some thoughts on the minds of the men and operators. But it took the ingenuity and might of Kwamivi and the team to foil the attack on the facility. When the attack was finally halted, kudos Kwamivi was identified and elevated to the status of the chief diver, chief of the security service and also responsible for the wellbeing of the owner and business tycoon of the facility.

Kwamivi, being the chief diver and leader of the security services required training from an external body. This was to make him efficient, effective and resourceful for his new role. An expert was invited into the country to access the security situation on the facility and offer training to the men and leaders. This initiative was comprehensive and herculeous and therefore was apt to propel the new chief to live up to the task as the previous chief diver and leader gave up the ghost in that abortive raid. He was offered a decent accommodation, fat salary, juicy incentives and pleasantries. Kwamivi who had come into the facility as a subjugate had now become a hero and a member of the top management of the facility. The once son of the drunkard, basic school drop-out, the truant fisher-folk and the subjugated boy, has found and realized his dream. The evil dream of the mother's lover meant only for the destruction of Kwamivi had now turned into a reality of hope, success and status.

## Advices
Creatures will until the end of time be constricted by revelation and occurrences of moments. Humans are unable to distinguish precisely talent and understanding from academic superiority. People may not have immense academic strength from their start but may excel in other disciplines of life. It is only the extraterrestrial world that has some admission to the future of inhabitants. Let us keep our vision and nurture them for our future. Let us be bold and dedicated to authority and service. Consult and bargain for the best if you can, make it work if you must, for if it must be done then it must be done well. People have the best resources and they need to keep them well natured and taped for the benefit of all. Welcome to the Eweland Kwamivi. You are the path to good performance.

## Symbolism of the root to the story
The tree roots colour has burnt umber, umber and ocher colour schemes that are obtained from the root's natural colour. The Acacia root is composed projections and perforations that suggest swift motion of aquatic poses. The cylindrical lower portion of the root composition offers a grand support base for the aquatic trade among the coastal and wet lands regions of the nation. The vertical projections that constitute the upper portion of the root structure have several projections and perforations that connect to the upward demand for human expertise in the fishing and aquatic trade. The combination of vertical projections and perforation offers the acacia root a potted cauliflower semblance and a gracious

posture. It provides a compact cylindrical lower portion on which sits the blossom roots heads. The piece projects a group of aquatic creatures springing from a pivoting base towards a concentrated direction to pursue their prey.

The upper most portion of the root structure has several vertical projections that connect to the base which serves as the receptacle to the creatures. These vertical projections represent the effort to survive after undertaking a diving activity from the basin into the water body. It suggests the action of a Crusader ready to step into some form of occupational and social liberation for the human race regardless of the lack of proper parental guidance and formal western education.

## CONCLUSION

Living beings that have existed and keep existing in the world has to propensity to be affected positively and negatively by their family and community. Creatures will until the end of time be slandered by revelation and occurrences of moments. Hence all persons that have the trust in their Almighty God and the cosmic authorities will be able to go over their predicament and became successful persons in their community, nation and the world. Let us keep faith in the Creator and the cosmic world and all shall be well.

# REFERENCE

1. The Mirror, Friday, June 24- 30, 2016, page 31, Relationship — Love Brewed in the Office, Dr. John Boakye.

2. Morning Devotion, Radio Maxx, July 16 2016, Joel Osten, Motivational Speaker and Preacher, Lakewood Church, Huston, USA.

3. LIVING WORD, Empire FM, June 10 2016, Dr. Mensa Otabil, Motivational Speaker and Preacher, International Central Gospel Church, Accra, Ghana.

4. Voice of Hope, Skyy Power FM, Mondays 5:00 am, Dr. Andrew L. Ewoo, Motivational Speaker and Preacher, Seventh Day Adventist Church, Accra, Ghana.

5. Encounter With The Truth, GTV, Sunday Mornings, Dr. Andrew L. Ewoo, Motivational Speaker and Preacher, Seventh Day Adventist Church, Accra, Ghana.

6. The Holistic Pediatrician: A Pediatrician's Comprehensive Guide To Safe and Effective Therapies for the 25 Most Common Ailment of Infants, Children and Adolescents: Kathi J. Kemper, Quill Publishers, New York, 2002,

7. Holistic Pediatrician: A Pediatrician's Comprehensive Guide To Safe and Effective Therapies for the 25 Most Common Ailment of Infants, Children and Adolescents: Kathi J. Kemper, Harper Perennial Publishers, New York, 1996,

8. Fundamentals of Wood Carving: David Asamani, , Andrews Amoako-Temeng, and Rex I. Akinruntan, , Takoradi, 2015.

9. Aesthetics and Appreciation of Tree Trunks and Branches into Sketches and Sculptures: Samuel Adentwi Bentum, Trafford Publishing Company, USA, 2014.

10. Sculpture; Technique, Form and Content A guide For Teachers: Judith Collins, Phiadon, London, 2007.

11. Sculpture Today: Judith Collins, Phiadon, London, 2007.

12. Wood Sculpture: Rood Ishn, The Lawheed Press, Athens, 1940.

13. Carstenson, Cecil C.: The Craft and Creation of Wood Sculpture, Edited by William S. Brown, Dover Publications, New York, 1981.

14. Bodunrin, P. O. (Ed.): The Philosophy in Africa: Trends and Perspectives, University of Ife Press, Ile-Ife, Nigeria, 1985.

15. Oladipo, Olusegun: Philosophy and the African Experience: The Contributions of Kwasi Wiredu/Olsugun Oladipo, Hope Publication, Ibadan, Nigeria, 1996.

16. Segy, Ladislas: African Sculpture and Writing, Journal of Human Relations,  Central State College (Wilberforce, Ohio), Quarterly Winter Issue, 1953.